*To anybody that did not know — I was part of this Memorial trip I know — JMattCrawford 6. Oct. 02*

# A Date With The
# Lonesome Lady
## A HIROSHIMA POW RETURNS

D1602800

# Lt. T. C. Cartwright
## PILOT, U.S. ARMY AIR FORCE

EAKIN PRESS ⬧ Austin, Texas

For CIP information,
please access:
www.loc.gov

FIRST EDITION
Copyright © 2002
By T.C. Cartwright
Published in the U.S.A.
By Eakin Press
A Division of Sunbelt Media, Inc.
P.O. Drawer 90159
Austin, Texas 78709-0159
email: eakinpub@sig.net
website: www.eakinpress.com
ALL RIGHTS RESERVED.
1   2   3   4   5   6   7   8   9
**1-57168-630-4**

*Dedicated to*

*the memory of the* Lonesome Lady *crew*

*who did not make it back*

# CONTENTS

Foreword                                                                    vii
Preface                                                                      ix

Chapter 1. A Lucky Kid Matures                                                1
*Growing Up, 1; Joining Up, 5; Flight Training, 6; Wings and
Bars, 9; The Liberator, 11; It Takes a Crew, 12; More
Training, 14*

Chapter 2. 494th Bombardment Group (H)                                       16
*Heading to the Pacific, 16; Assignment to Combat, 18; Moving
Closer, 21; Initiation, 23; A Date with the* Lonesome Lady,
*24; Damn Rough Mission, 26; POW, 28; Interrogation Center,
32; Strange Music, 33; Liberated, 37; Waiting . . . Hoping,
40; Official Responses, 42; Roy Pedersen, 42; Durden Looper,
44; Jim Ryan, 45; Ralph Neal, 45; Hugh Atkinson, 47; Julius
Molnar, 48; Relevant Stories, 49; The* Taloa, *49; The*
Haruna, *50; A Small Piece of the "Lady" Who Flew Back
Home as a Peace Dove, 50; The Indefatigable Mr. Mori, 52;
Conclusions, 54; Reflections, 55*

Chapter 3. A Return to Hiroshima     59
  *Earlier Visits, 59; Peace Offerings, 61; A Pilgrimage, 62;
  POW Memorial, 64; Hiroshima Haunts, 66; Hiroshima
  Museum, 67;* Taloa *Crash Site, 69; BB* Haruna *Revisited,
  70; Memories Revisited, 72; Memories Expanded, 73; Dream
  Never Dreamed, 78; Unexpected Meetings, 82; Winding
  Down, 83; Added Meeting, 85; Reflected Reflections, 88*

Epilogue     91

Appendix     95
References     99

# FOREWORD

The World War II experiences of Thomas Campbell Cartwright described in this account were unique among those of millions who served in the armed forces of the United States. For almost fifty years he was reticent to discuss his experiences, declining requests for interviews—particularly at times near the anniversary of the dropping of the atomic bomb on Hiroshima. Encouraged by family and friends to do so, he recently wrote his recollections of the events that transpired between July 28 and early September 1945.

Thomas C. Cartwright is a graduate of Clemson University (B.S. 1948) and of Texas A&M University (M.S. 1949; Ph.D. 1954). After receiving his doctorate, he joined the faculty of Texas A&M University and the Texas Agricultural Experiment Station where he and I were colleagues for more than thirty years. There, he distinguished himself in the field of population genetics, applying his experience particularly to the improvement of beef cattle breeding. He introduced the techniques of systems analysis to animal breeding and livestock production; he is recognized as an authority in the evaluation of hybrid vigor and breed characteristics in crossing cattle. Dr. Cartwright has participated in many international programs for the improvement of animal agriculture and in the education of a generation of agricultural scientists for developing countries.

In addition to having distinguished himself in research, Dr. Cartwright has been teacher and mentor for numerous graduate students and is an active and conscientious citizen of the university as Professor Emeritus.

J. M. Prescott
Professor Emeritus
Texas A&M University

# PREFACE

The core beginning of this book was drafted in 1992 and revised and corrected in 1995 but was distributed to only a few people. Some facts and observations were added as requested by Dave Rogers, Historian, 494th Bombardment Group (H), Seventh Air Force, and as I thought appropriate for a historical document that might be of interest to my family, Bill Abel, families of my deceased crew members, close friends, and perhaps some people interested in WW II history.

After the first rewriting, two Japanese gentlemen provided me with new information that was relevant for several corrections and additions, which prompted a second rewriting in 1998. One of these men, Mr. Keiichi Muranaka, a naval recruit who witnessed my B-24 bomber being shot down made significant contributions for this account. The other man, Mr. Shigeaki Mori, was an eight-year-old boy in Hiroshima when the atomic bomb was dropped and is now a historian in that city. He first contacted me in 1995 and has since gone to extraordinary efforts to find facts and artifacts, by conducting personal interviews and locating obscure documents related to the fateful mission of the *Lonesome Lady* and its crew. I am grateful to them and wish to acknowledge their past efforts and, as you will see, their continuing efforts.

The efforts and accomplishments of Mr. Muranaka and Mr. Mori were truly impressive, and I became interested in meeting them in person, so I took them up on their invitations to visit them. I wanted to visit places where, due to their efforts, a memorial plaque and monument were placed in memory of my crew, plus, of course, places where I and my crew had been captured and held in and around Hiroshima. My wife, Carolyn, younger son, Dr. Pat Cartwright, and Mr. Matt Crawford, president of the 494th Bombardment Group (H) Association, all asked to join me. My return visit to Hiroshima was an event which will always be vivid in my memory. Therefore, to add a report of this trip was of compelling interest to me, and in a sense, it completed the story of my experience beginning over a half century ago. Several people had encouraged me to write a book about my Japanese experience and related events. The time seemed to be right, so I began editing and writing.

I have made an effort to report only factual material, documented where possible. However, I often had to rely on my memory going back a half century or more and on secondhand accounts. I attempted to make clear where either my memory or one or more removed accounts were the sole source of information. There are passages recounting my personal feelings or expressing my opinions that are stated without caveat.

Perhaps I should add the motivation expressed in the post WW I motto: Lest We Forget.

T. C. Cartwright
2001

# Chapter One

# A LUCKY KID MATURES

## Growing Up

The town of York was mainly a cotton mill and agricultural town in the Piedmont hills of South Carolina in the Great Depression era of the late 1920s and 1930s. Although beginning to fade a bit, it still held to the manners and traditions of its past. Everyone was expected to say "yes sir" and "yes ma'am" (often contracted to yesuh or yesum) to older adult whites and to call the "colored" people by their first name regardless of age. Everyone was expected to go to Sunday school and church; the Presbyterians of Scotch-Irish decent predominated. The schools had eleven grades and were segregated between whites and "coloreds." Among the white kids there were clearly recognized distinctions based on their family status; the more genteel town folk and the country folk who owned their land tended to exclude the cotton mill workers and sharecroppers in their social circle. Unemployment and underemployment were high, and money was scarce in most families and almost nonexistent in many.

I was born into this setting in 1924 and named Thomas Campbell Cartwright. By 1932/33 I was old enough to recognize

1

that times were hard when two uncles who had gone to big cities came back to live with their in-law parents and got WPA (Work Projects Administration) jobs. My father (Daddy) campaigned and voted right and was appointed postmaster, a political appointment, in 1932. His steady income combined with depressed prices provided means for Daddy to buy a small farm and build a house at the edge of town. My older brother Perry and I raised chickens, milked cows, and I raised and fitted a state grand champion steer. At twelve years of age I applied for a driver's license, passed the minor exam, paid the fifty-cent fee, and became a legal driver. These were fertile grounds for gaining experience at a young age, but at this time in my life I could not possibly imagine what lay ahead or understand how a work ethic and self-reliance might become a valuable background asset.

Daddy expected a lot in terms of work and was strict about such things as manners and respect for traditions; he did not change easily. He had met Ruth Patton in France, where he was an artillery officer and she was a nurse in WW I, and they were married in 1920 after coming home from the war. Ruth was from California and had grown up on a ranch overlooking Salinas Valley, so the move to York, a traditional southern town, was a cultural shock. As one might guess, a young lady who joined the Army Nurse Corps for overseas service in those days was venturesome and self-confident. She was strong and vigorous and did a lot of the work of the small farm. Dr. Barron, the local family doctor who was obese but astute, noted that Ruth was the only woman that he ever saw hoeing with a mattock. Racial intolerance and social status were foreign to Ruth and, although her actions were passive, it was clear that her feelings and desires were not to look down on anyone, and Perry and I tended to absorb and share her feelings. Mother allowed us a great deal of freedom in choosing friends and in our activities. School attendance was mandatory, but fair to good grades were accepted and little emphasis was put on checking homework or scholastic achievement.

By the time we had finished high school, Perry and I had been in and out of a lot of minor mischief and adventures typical—but also several not so typical—of teenage boys. One was to buy a truck and scour the countryside for cattle to resell at the cattle auction close to the city of Charlotte thirty-two miles away. This venture required lots of initiative and bargaining, but for novices it was exciting yet only marginally profitable. On one trip through Charlotte we stopped at Hielbein's Junk Yard to buy a piece of scrap iron to fix the cattle bed of the truck damaged by crowding too many cattle against the side boards. While standing dismayed at the price of the piece of scrap iron, Mr. Hielbein volunteered to give us this piece of scrap iron since we were so enterprising. Then after saying "Just call me Hy," in a confidential tone he suggested that he would pay top price if we could find loads of scrap iron to bring in to his yard. Inquiries at a few farms revealed that the farmers placed little value on their piles of old plow shares, ancient, long-abandoned tractors, and other worn-out farm implements that lay around most farm yards. We learned from trial and error and lots of bruises how to dismantle an old tractor with wrenches, a sledge hammer and cold chisel, to separate the different types of metals, and then cash in. A favorite find was to learn that the farmer had gone to town and then tell the wife that we would clean up that trash pile in her side yard and give her five dollars to boot. It sometimes paid off well—the scrap iron was loaded quickly and the entrepreneurs got out of sight quickly. We even got so bold as to try to bargain with Hy over the price that he paid us for a pound of scrap, but we were way out of our league. We made "good money" for teenagers, but Japan was the main benefactor. Their demand had shot prices up for scrap iron, but we were mostly unaware of the economic and political issues surrounding scrap iron that prevailed at the time.

After high school and a year at the University of South Carolina, Perry had reached seventeen years, was restless, and joined the Canadian Air Force in 1940. I was still in high school, enjoying life, and sometimes took advantage of the free rein that my parents gave me. I was mischievous but not really bad, mostly doing such things as taking my typewriter apart in typing class, or slipping out of study hall to explore the attic of the ancient school building and then enticing a friend and two girls to join in the challenge of not getting caught. Once I almost got caught when the principal happened up at a spot under the trap door just after I had crawled down from the attic. He reprimanded me for having such dirty hands. I pleaded that my agriculture class had been examining soil to classify types and was on my way to wash up. It was true that I was on my way to wash up, but the soil classification class had been the day before.

I hung out with some boys and girls that were friends, but I tried to be friendly with all of my classmates and got elected class president. I did not go steady, although I dated several different girls, but I never dated the girl that I liked best, Carolyn, because she had other boyfriends. I just tried to join in groups that included her in games we played and in just hanging out.

After high school I was sent to spend a year with Uncle Tom, Aunt Tress, and their young son Tom in order to attend Amarillo Junior College, so that I could establish residency in Texas in order to study veterinary medicine at Texas A&M College. On December 7, 1941, I was watching a picture show when the film stopped and the manager came on stage and read the headlines of a special edition of the Amarillo paper: "Japs Attack Pearl Harbor." I went home immediately and in my youthful naivete asked Uncle Tom if this attack was serious. He assured me that it was of utmost gravity.

Perhaps three were just too many Tom Cartwrights under one roof and the war times were unsettling, but for whatever reason I wanted out and headed back home to York after the first year. Although I had announced my intentions to return to York, I planned to actually depart on a day that Uncle Tom was gone on a business trip. When I told Aunt Tress that I was hitch hiking back to South Carolina via Canada to see brother Perry, she was very much dismayed. She was not free and easy like Ruth, my mother, so I left quickly before she could protest too much, caught the city bus to the edge of town, and luckily soon caught one ride all the way to Oklahoma City. After many different rides, I reached Detroit, entered Canada, and wound my way through London and on to Dunville, west of Toronto, where I found Perry at his RCAF base. We visited for a weekend, and then I headed south. Rides were of shorter distance and I had to wait longer for a pickup in Canada, but when I got to Pittsburgh after a couple of days of thumbing, lady luck rolled up again. A private trucker was heading south to pick up produce and stopped to pick me up. As I climbed aboard, the trucker was disappointed to find that I was so young, but when I told him that I had driven a similar truck and had a truck driver's license, he tried letting me drive for a while. Apparently satisfied, he outlined the route and went to sleep. When we reached Charlotte I got off and was home in a couple of hours.

That summer back at home I finished up the scrap iron business, sold the truck, and just spent time hanging out. In the fall I entered Clemson College in a premed program since a preveterinary program was not available. I had no idea about real study and my efforts were uninspired. Having traveled to California to visit my mother's family, to Florida for a few days, and now to Texas and Canada, I had a wanderlust. I yearned to see more of the world and to have some excitement that York did not appear likely to provide. By that time, 1942, the war effort was full blown, so the obvious opportunity to escape from boring college and the small-town environment was to "join up"; also it was the patriotic thing to do, which I did take seriously. I had had enough experience to develop a lot of self-confidence and was not apprehensive about the military.

## Joining Up

What could be more exciting than the Air Corps? I was eighteen years old and eligible, so I applied for acceptance and passed the physical and other exams, and was inducted in February of 1943, assigned to report to my first post: Miami Beach, Florida—boy, I thought, what a deal!

This first post for basic training was at a small hotel, The Anchor, surrounded by many large hotels filled with other Air Corps inductees. We were given uniforms, underclothes, shoes, etc., and taught about NCO and CO ranks, which rank to salute, how to march, and other very basic military things which I already knew from the military training at Clemson College. What I had not foreseen was the geographical mixture of inductees with whom I would be in close contact. All the inductees in my outfit had last names that started with either A, B or C, and I was now either Thomas or Tom Cartwright. Some of this new band of recruits had unbelievable accents like I had never heard before. I really did not believe that the ones from the Bronx would have the accents that they did. But my southern drawl was, of course, natural and proper in my opinion. Many were a lot bigger and some used abusive language that I was not accustomed to hearing directed to another person. Also, I learned a lot of "army" language from the sergeant in charge and his corporal assistant. My temperament and past experiences were such that I adjusted well, at least for a small-town southern boy.

I was overwhelmed by Miami Beach and went exploring on every off day. One Saturday I ventured into the Sands Theater to see *Casablanca*. The auditorium was amazing in size and the seats were padded. It took a while for me to figure out that the guy with the muted flashlight was trying to escort me to a seat. The novelty soon wore off, and I began to wonder about learning to fly.

Orders were posted, and I finally pushed through the crowd to find the name of Thomas C. Cartwright posted to be transferred to Center College, Danville, Kentucky. I thought: What kind of flight school is this college? It turned out to be a holding place where basic math and other subjects were presented. A few flights in a Piper Cub were designed apparently to keep us mollified. Mostly, I learned to drink beer; age did not seem to matter there for anyone in uniform. Next was Maxwell Field, Alabama, which was considered to be the academy for the Army Air Corps, and classification was now flight cadet, a big boost to morale. The most memorable things there were military protocol to the extreme, physical conditioning, and being barked at, dog-style, by other flight cadets as our platoon marched or jogged by. Our platoon was designated as K-9.

## Flight Training

Orders were posted to Primary Flight School. I shipped out by train to Darr Aero Tech, Albany, Georgia, which was a private contract school with a few Air Corps officers, all "retreads" to maintain army discipline, and civilian flight instructors. At last, I was in real training to become a pilot, to advance to the next level—or "wash out." The planes were bi-wing Stearman PT-19s, which were very sturdy and highly maneuverable with two tandem seats in open cockpits. The PT-19 had two major faults; one was that the radial engine had to be started by a swift turn of the propeller by hand or by cranking the fly wheel by hand up to a whining sound and then engaging it. The other fault, at least for a novice, was the narrow spacing between the wheels of the landing gear which was conducive to ground loops. After an instruction flight or two, I felt comfortable with the plane and flying with my assigned instructor sitting in the cockpit behind me. I soloed after ten hours of instruction; soloing was an achievement that remains vivid in my memory.

Now I was free to fly solo and could not imagine anything more fun than taking off and landing and in between practicing loops, stalls, spins, and snap rolls. The instructor had pressed on us several safety measures: in case of emergency don't try to land in one of the numerous pecan orchards that looked grassy smooth from the air; don't get lost, always keep up with where you are; and be cautious of the Stearman's tendency to ground loop when landing because of the narrow landing gear. On my last check flight, everything had gone well, and I was in the last critical phase of the check flight: landing. I was being careful to enter the flight pattern correctly for landing when the instructor checking me out yelled through the intercom tube: "You are stalling way too high, give it power, nose down, don't, don't, don't!" After the shock of these weird instructions being shouted at me, I realized that the instructor was watching the plane in front of us landing. Sure enough, it was stalling. The plane dropped to the ground from about fifty feet up, crashed into the ground, and went into a ground loop. The cadet pilot who was soloing was pretty badly bruised—and washed out.

Gratefully, I was advanced to the next stage of flying, but having watched an accident happen gave me some pause to think about something that scarcely had entered my mind: flying was dangerous. Flight training became more serious business as I advanced to basic flight training at the Greenville, Mississippi, Army Air Corps Base. The exposure was now to Air Corps officers who could chew out an errant cadet with blistering, humiliating language. The planes were BT-7s with a single engine and variable pitch props, again with two tandem seats but with enclosed cockpits. I concentrated on learning and practicing and, after adjusting to the intimidating officers, enjoyed the training experience because it involved flying. On my final flight check with a captain, I went through takeoff, landing, and maneuvers well except for one.

The captain called for a steep, level turn to the right. This was a piece of cake, I thought. But then something did not seem quite right, and I felt the plane shudder a bit—this was unusual. The captain barked, "I don't know how you did that turn without stalling—didn't you learn to advance the throttle as you enter a steep turn?" I had never gotten less than "excellent" rating on flying and was apprehensive when I faced the captain for a debriefing in his office after the flight. The captain always had a serious, stern look on his face and was feared by the cadets. He apparently sensed my tenseness and after looking over my record deviated from his usual critique. He would usually leave the trembling cadets in the dark while he critiqued their performance until his last statement when he informed them either that "you passed" or "you failed and have washed out of flight training." The captain said, "Mr. Cartwright, you have passed, but if you had stalled in that tight turn, I would have had a hard decision to make." Mr. Cartwright responded with, "I know that the throttle must be advanced going into a turn, especially a tight turn but..." The captain reverted to his usual demeanor, interrupting with, "It doesn't matter what you know when flying under pressure. All that matters is what you do." "Yes, sir." Hooray! Another excellent rating, but with a minus attached, and off to advanced flight training.

When orders were posted the cadets were more anxious than usual; the next post indicated whether they had been chosen for bomber or for fighter training. Thomas C. Cartwright was posted across Mississippi to the Columbus Army Air Corps Base for advanced bomber training. Those who had washed out knew it by now but, even if dejected, were anxious to see their next post, which would indicate whether they would have another chance to be an officer in some other capacity or remain in a non-commissioned rank.

Advanced training was more challenging, introducing twin engines, night flying, radio communication, and navigation. Two throttles, twice as many instruments, and "dead reckoning" navigation were Cadet Cartwright's "cup of tea," even though he missed the acrobatics that his comrades sent to fighter training no doubt enjoyed. My fellow cadets were the sixth mix of young men that I had experienced, and I had learned how to quickly pick friends. The worst part of advanced training was being assigned as pilot or copilot with a cadet who was obnoxious or incompetent.

About midway through advanced training I was assigned to fly copilot late in the morning with a lieutenant instructor whose mission was to go up to about 6,000 feet on a weather reconnaissance mission to check the weather for the afternoon flights, since a front was expected to blow in. The lieutenant made his observations and reported in by radio as we returned to the field. Several other planes were coming in from morning flights, and after waiting our turn we entered the landing flight pattern. We had made the last turn onto the approach when the plane landing just in front of us drew our attention. "Good Lord, not again," I said to myself, sitting in the copilot seat. The trick of landing is to stall (lose lift) just before the wheels touch the runway, but the training plane that was about to land in front of us was stalling out too high just as the Stearman I had witnessed crashing in primary flight training. Its wings wobbled and it dropped hard to the runway with the left wing drooping. The left wheel hit hard, broke off, and crashed through the plywood wing and wing gas tank. It burst into flames immediately.

The lieutenant flying as pilot was stunned at the horrible sight. Cadet Cartwright would of course not think of telling an officer instructor to do something, but I was yelling to myself "Go around, Go around!" and had started to reach for the throttles. The lieutenant had recovered, however, and was already advancing the throttles and lifting the nose to go around. After circling for about an hour, we were cleared to land cross-wind on the only other runway.

I rushed to the ready room to learn who had been caught in the burning plane. One was a good buddy and the other I knew only casually. Two cadets accompanied each body to their homes.

### Wings and Bars

I had now just passed my teen years in March of 1944. Though only twenty years old, the tough training and the experience of witnessing two accidents led to a maturity that belied my boyish appearance. I became more contemplative about the serious business of Air Corps flying. A few weeks after witnessing the crash of a plane incinerating two classmates, I graduated from Flight Cadet to Second Lieutenant Cartwright, a great boost to morale and ego. My dreams were coming true: a commissioned officer in a neat uniform, but best of all genuine silver wings on my chest. Almost every other student in my graduating class who had gotten an "Excellent" rating was awarded a Good Conduct Medal. Although I never tested flight instructions and rules, I sometimes did, too often, test other regulations—such as getting caught sleeping through reveille and failing to salute an officer. Even though the failure to salute was inadvertent, this was a serious breach of conduct expected of an officer candidate. The first medals that we were eligible to receive were the Good Conduct Medals, but my friend that I nicknamed "Big Wheel" Carpenter, from "Big D" (Dallas) and I were the only ones who did not get the privilege of having a medal to pin to our new officer uniforms.

Before reporting to duty at Harlingen, Texas, my first assignment as pilot, I had a week's leave, which was a great delight because it gave me the chance to show off in my officer's uniform with wings pinned on my chest and lieutenant bars on my epaulets. Back in York I shook hands with many older men on Main Street and even more at church. More important than feasting on the admiration of the older citizens of York and especially of my parents was to go see Carolyn at Queens College in Charlotte. We met on our date in the parlor of the main administration building, which was closely chaperoned with the aid of many mirrors. We strolled out to sit on a bench on the well-groomed lawns. Soon our eyes met and we knew what the other had in their heart. We kissed, and there was no question from then on about our love for each other. My head was spinning, and I was not sure that I could drive the thirty-two miles back to York. Carolyn was no doubt wondering how to write Stanley, the boyfriend she was leaving, that she was really in love with his best friend Tommy, who had just come to see her.

**The Liberator**

My first post as an officer and pilot was to Harlingen Army Air Base to train as copilot of the B-24 four-engine bomber, the Liberator. While a cadet at Maxwell Field, I had often walked out on the flight line as close as the guards would allow to observe the B-24 Liberators, newly built and posted there for pilot training. The B-24 was a replacement for the venerable B-17 Flying Fortress with faster cruising speed, longer range, and heavier payload. Its mass-produced numbers, 18,000, exceeded that of any other military plane. Even without a bomb payload and armor, it was somewhat difficult to fly, but this was a challenge. Mastering this beast became a passion, and I studied the manuals and went out to the flight line on off days just to look over this most modern of bombers with a newly designed "Davis" wing with an impressive 110-foot wing span for high efficiency along with four 1200 HP, 14-cylinder radial engines built by the prestigious Pratt and Whitney Company. I could hardly believe that I was entrusted to fly this wonder that reportedly cost a quarter of a million dollars. When anyone called it the Flying Box Car, I took offense. I was intent on learning to fly this complex aircraft, but also seemed to have a natural affinity for flying the big plane. Landing was the most difficult part, and I took pride in my ability to "grease it in" for impeccable landings. Another excellent rating and I was privileged to go directly on to pilot training rather than being assigned to a crew as copilot, which was unusual for a twenty-year-old who looked more like he was eighteen. Feeling more responsibility coming my way, I decided that it would be well to keep up with the war in Europe and the Pacific, so I began to read the papers more closely; the reports of air strikes and planes lost were the focus of my closest attention.

I went back to Maxwell Field, close to Montgomery, Alabama, for training to fly in the left seat of those planes I had admired as a cadet. Two intense months were spent practicing takeoffs, landings, and navigation as well as a lot of classroom training about the plane in combat, such as loading bombs, high-altitude flying, fuel conservation measures, and emergency procedures such as ditching and surviving in a life raft.

There was some off-time, and I flirted with a cute girl working in the officers' mess and took her to a movie one Saturday night. She asked if she could wear my high school ring just to show the other girls. What young and inexperienced man could refuse a plea from an attractive young lady? That was a poor decision much to my regret—it was the last I ever saw of that ring.

The next week I was given a final check ride with a major, a veteran who had earned his return home after flying missions in Europe. He flew in the copilot's seat without saying a word until after we landed, parked, and shut off the engines. He chewed me out rather severely, a kid with lieutenant bars, for appearing overconfident, which "can get you in trouble after having flown a B-24 for only a few hours as pilot." A chewing out was probably standard operating procedure for the major with the purpose of impressing on young pilots that they still had lots to learn and needed a lot more experience. I hoped that the "Exc+" the major placed in the performance rating column would help erase the "Exc-" received in basic training.

Now I was ready to be assigned a crew and as pilot I would be commander of the crew. About time, I thought. It was already August 1944 and fighting was fierce in Europe and the Pacific on the ground, in the air, and on the sea. The next post was AAF Base in Lemoore, California, to be assigned a crew, but I had seven days' leave (the orders stated "7 days delay in travel") to return to York to visit my family and go to church again in full uniform with my wings attached to my chest and second lieutenant bars on the epaulets. But the most important thing was to get to see Carolyn again at college in nearby Charlotte.

### It Takes a Crew

With thoughts of Carolyn having taken priority in his mind the past days, Lieutenant Cartwright, pilot and "AP Comdr" now directed his thoughts to being assigned a combat crew. A B-24 required ten men to fill all of the positions needed for combat. Where would they have come from? What would they be like personally and how competent, etc.? Those questions were soon answered as I met my officers: Lt. Durden Looper, copilot from Arkansas; Lt. Roy Pedersen, navigator from Iowa; and Lt. James Ryan from New York. Then the NCOs stood in a crowd in front of a sergeant who called out names one by one along with the name of their crew commander—who stood at the edge of the crowd and held up his hand when his name was called to identify himself. In turn I greeted my men. The ones who remained with the crew until the last flight were: Sgt. Hugh Atkinson, radio operator from Seattle; Staff Sgt. William Abel, gunner from Colorado; PFC John Long, gunner from Pennsylvania; Sgt. Buford Ellison, gunner later to take over as flight engineer, from Texas. The flight engineer and one gunner position were filled by several different people at various times.

Before our crew had barely learned the names of each other, we were off to Muroc AAF in the Mohave Desert for combat crew training. There we became friends, not distinguishing between COs and NCOs except as required. We flew navigation missions, high-altitude practice at 20,000 feet, where it was -20 degrees Fahrenheit and required oxygen masks, and bomb runs over targets marked in the desert.

On a gunnery practice mission over Death Valley the gunners shot at a target towed by a B-26 twin-engine light bomber. This exercise was close to the real thing; actually, it was a lot of fun since the target did not shoot back. We were flying in formation with five other planes as we would in real combat. When the lead plane called cease-fire, all the gunners cleared and stowed their fifty-caliber machine guns—except for one errant gunner on a plane off our right wing. This careless top turret gunner failed to clear his hot guns and left his turret for a cup of coffee on the flight deck. The bullets began to "cook" off, and Corporal Long reported over the intercom from his waist gunner position that he had spotted smoke puffs coming from the top turret of the plane flying off our right wing. I immediately radioed the offending plane and the errant guns soon stopped firing.

Unfortunately, one or more of the errant bullets had found its way to the oil pan of one of our engines. Copilot Looper had noted that the oil pressure in number three engine was dropping and watched as it got close to zero. He reported this to me, and I ordered Looper to feather the prop to reduce drag and turn off the ignition. I immediately left the formation, radioed in the problem to the tower, and headed straight for our home airfield. The B-24 could fly and maintain its altitude with one engine feathered if it was not loaded with fuel and bombs. Nevertheless, the tower instructed us by radio to land at Edwards AAF, which was located on Muroc Dry Lake and was closer than home base and much less crowded. Navigator Pedersen quickly figured the correct heading, and Looper and I calmly took it in with three engines—no problem except it helped having two people on the controls to help overcome the pull of two engines against one. After landing, taxiing and following a jeep marked with a big sign on back reading "Follow Me," we saw to our astonishment a sleek-looking plane sitting on the tarmac with a big air scoop in the nose instead of a propeller. When we taxied to our parking spot behind the guide jeep and shut down the remaining engines, an officer boarded, gathered the crew on the flight deck, and told us that whatever we might have seen was top secret and not to mention it to anyone—not even to one another. He then bellowed, "That's an order, understand?" Our crew was ushered directly into a bus and back to Muroc AAF. What we had seen was, of course, a prototype jet fighter.

The poor gunner who failed to clear his guns was up for court-martial and I, as pilot, was brought in to testify before the group of officers holding court. A colonel asked me to describe the incident from my perspective. I did so tersely, military-style, relating Corporal Long's sighting the smoke puffs, reporting it to the offending plane, Lieutenant Looper noting the oil pressure dropping, feathering the engine, radioing in, and landing as instructed without incident. The colonel asked if that was all and I replied, "Yes, sir, we followed the routine for flying and landing with one engine out." Perhaps our crew's alertness and the cool and efficient manner in which we followed through earned a "Superior" rating at Muroc Army Air Field.

### More Training

The next orders read that we were transferred to the Fourth Air Force Processing Station, Hamilton Field, California, for overseas movement. We were ready to go and excited, arriving on February 10, 1945, only to be reassigned on February 12 to report to Langley Field, Virginia. We were based there for two months to become trained as a radar crew. Lt. Frank Lones was assigned to our crew as the "mickey" operator.

This was exciting, being on the cutting edge of scientific developments applied to air warfare, but it lacked the excitement of going to combat. We mostly flew missions to give Lones practice with his radar equipment, leaving a lot of free time. The only exciting moment was when we were coming in from a night training mission and flew over the field. It was hazy with fog, but the runways were clearly visible looking straight down through the fog. More dense fog moved in quickly as we entered the landing flight pattern, but we could still see the runway lights. On the final approach as we let down into the fog and were looking through the fog horizontally, everything went blank—we could see nothing except our landing lights muffled by the fog. A quick decision: go around and wait for the fog to clear, which might not be until the next morning, or fly on in, hoping that we would get a glimpse of the runway before we flew into the ground. We kept going, flying by instruments, believing it was our only choice. Runway lights suddenly appeared just in time to allow us to line up with the runway and level out for a normal landing. We cautiously felt our way back to the flight line to park, and Looper and I looked at one another and could tell that each thought it best to not discuss with the others that we were flying blind for a short while.

The best part of being at Langley Field was getting a three-day pass which was long enough for me to visit Carolyn and my family, and Carolyn to visit her cousin who lived close by in Norfolk. We enjoyed the seafood, went to movies, and just sat around with each other, smooching when we were alone. It was then that we knew we were meant for each other and considered ourselves engaged without ever saying so.

While on a date we learned of President Roosevelt's death, which saddened us but also troubled us; we did not know then whether Truman could effectively take over presidential leadership in such demanding times.

# Chapter Two

# 494TH BOMBARDMENT GROUP (H)

### Heading to the Pacific

In April we were off again across the continent, flyers traveling by train to the AAF Base Unit, Salinas, California. This was just a stopover to pick up a new radar-equipped B-24 J on the way to Mather Field, Sacramento, to be posted overseas. Finally, we thought—but where?

The orders read to deliver aircraft and crew to the CO, Barking Sands Air Combat Replacement Center, Kauai, Hawaii. We were authorized to make variations as necessary to complete this mission. We were exuberant, gathered our gear and a few illicit supplies, and took off for Hickam Field, Hawaii, on April 15, 1945. It was a long flight and the first real test to fly as economically as possible starting with full fuel tanks, but the most stress was on Pedersen to navigate us, mostly by dead reckoning since long-range radio was blacked out to that island in the Pacific. We were right on course and, with a small adjustment after sighting landfall, headed for Hickam Field, entered the flight landing pattern, and landed. It was a circus of air traffic.

After landing, I started taxiing to the tarmac parking space designated for us, and the tower yelled: "B-24 get your butt moving—get going!" I thought that I was already taxiing at maximum safe speed but moved the throttles up a notch. We were allowed to rest, get our plane fueled, and then pushed out. I was amazed, overwhelmed actually, to encounter at the desk where I signed in and out a dozen or so colonels and generals standing around waiting for clearance to fly out. Some were actually hitchhiking but none wanted to go to Kauai or, I would guess, fly in a B-24 bomber. Our clearance was simple and we took off for Barking Sands Air Combat Replacement Center on the next island over.

Approaching the island of Kauai, which we had already heard was a dream island, we diverted flight just a bit to confirm that it was indeed what we had been told, a picture postcard island, and then landed at Barking Sands Airfield. This assignment was of course just a holding place where we were waiting to be sent on as a replacement crew. We took advantage of this place, thumbing around the island, swimming, and testing the "barking sands" along the beach adjoining the air field. We would jump off the top of the sand cliff, and as we impacted the sand it made a sound a bit like the bark of a dog. Some of the crew went one way and others another way, usually mixed CO and NCO, around the island with little duties to perform. Jim Ryan usually went his own way, and we learned later that he and a young lady, Mary Paragua, who lived in the closest town, had become quite fond of each other. Mary did later marry but always remembered Jim and still corresponds with his brother Francis.

We tried to stay out of serious trouble and managed to do so with one close call. Roy Pedersen and I were walking around the compound the first week, just getting acquainted, when a major pulled up in a jeep and told us in a very official tone that we were not allowed in the Officer's Club until we had been there a week (why this restriction existed is unknown to me). "Yes, sir, we know that." "Then why the hell are you walking straight toward it?" We watched him drive off and park not too far away in a lot we figured was by the Officer's Club. Roy, always a gentleman and conservative in nature, was a little mad. After a pause he asked me if I had ever ridden in a jeep, which was still a fairly new military vehicle at that time. I said no, and we both took a brush-covered path off the road toward the parking lot and saw that the keys were still in the major's jeep. We jumped in and took off, and after a short spin we abandoned it at the main headquarters building. The foolishness of this stunt sunk in and we laid low for a while. Later, we always had someone scout the Officer's Club before going in and always left by the back door if we saw some brass coming in from the parking lot—they always had jeeps.

### Assignment to Combat

The progress of the war as the allies invaded Europe and progressed toward Germany was, of course, big news but was not celebrated as much in the Pacific as in the U.S. and Europe. It was now May 1945 and we had only flown a couple of training missions and anxiously awaited combat assignment. Finally, we were posted to the 494th Bombardment Group (Heavy), 7th Air Force, based on Angaur Island of the Palau Group of the Carolines.

We took off stopping first at the tiny atoll of Johnston Island for fuel. Just after takeoff, John Long, ever alert, reported from his waist gunner's position that there was a bad oil leak on the right wing. Ellison, acting as our engineer, raced back to look out the side window and reported that it was pouring out oil. We could not proceed on our flight with a serious oil leak, which I judged to be too serious to allow us time to fly around the island in circles in order to use up fuel to reduce our plane to a "safe landing gross weight." So we circled back and landed with full tanks of gas. This was a little dicey, but we landed OK even if a little heavily and managed to stop before the end of the runway without burning our brakes to the point of smoking. The firetrucks were standing by, and the ground crew came out to inspect. They filled the oil tank and we were given instructions to take off again. I was not going to accept that instruction until Ellison, who was on the wing watching every step, reported that the trouble was that the ground crew had failed to replace the oil cap. He also reported that the brakes did not feel excessively hot, so we took off again, landing at Kwajalien for a brief rest and then on to Saipan.

We were billeted overnight on Saipan, and even though exhausted, we watched in awe as a flight of B-29s were landing—presumably coming in from a raid on the Japanese main islands.

That was the first time that we had seen these new, pressurized, long-distance bombers that were twice as big as B-24s. That is, all of us watched from outside our tents except Jim Ryan, who sneaked out and went looking for his brother Francis, a Marine stationed on Saipan. Neither Francis nor I to this day know how Jim found him, but he did by chance happen on to his outfit and had a few hours visit with him.

If any of our crew had ever known even the names Caroline Islands and Palau Group, much less Angaur, from some geography lessons, we had forgotten them. So we were anxious as Pedersen headed us for this small atoll of the archipelago to see our first combat base. We had been briefed about possible anti-aircraft fire from small islands and enemy ships en route, so we avoided some small islands close to Angaur. This reminded us that we were entering the war zone. As usual, Pedersen was right on target after a correction for a wind change. From the air it was a small, inviting-looking tropical island.

As we let down on the final approach, the white coral runway startled Looper and me with its brightness. I did not like to land with my dark glasses on and had taken them off, but with this intense glare, I reflexively grabbed them out of my flight suit pocket and put them back on. The landing of a replacement crew was no doubt watched by more than the usual observers, and luckily, in spite of the distracting glare, we greased in one of our smoothest landings.

Arriving on May 30, 1945, we were met rather perfunctorily, taken to our quarters (tents), and given some information about where things were. Then we officers went to report in to the brass who gave us a briefing about the place and told us what was expected of us and what we could and could not do around the island. We were designated as crew 42B and assigned to the 866th Squadron and told to wait further orders.

After a few days we were checked out on a short flight by the CO of the 866th. Angaur was definitely an outpost with crude facilities, such as eating out of mess kits, pit latrines etc. But what else could one want on a tropical paradise island seven, degrees north of the equator? We were about 2,000 miles directly south of Japan. We enjoyed swimming off a beach close to our tent, but also did hiking and target practicing with our new

.45-caliber sidearms. When they were available and in the mood, we talked with the veteran crews to learn as much about combat missions as we could. The COs and NCOs of our crew still got together for recreation and bull sessions.

The 494th had begun arriving at Angaur, following somewhat the same path as we took from Barking Sands, in October 1944. They flew bombing missions to many of the smaller islands such as Koror, Yap, and Truk, but the major target was the Philippines, including Corregidor. The 494th flew eighty-three missions over the Philippines and received commendations from several generals including Douglas MacArthur. By January 1945, the Japanese Navy was largely destroyed or crippled to the extent of being pretty much restricted to the inland seas of Japan, but not entirely. The kamikaze attack tactic had been started during the Okinawa battle since the Japanese Air Force was now very limited in planes, pilots, and fuel and had begun to hoard their planes for these attacks on our transport and fighting ships. These suicide missions were very effective and demoralizing to our troops, especially the U.S. Navy. Therefore, the strategy that the 494th began to employ was to attempt to destroy Japanese aircraft on the ground along with their airfields and supplies, thus destroying as much as possible of the planes and facilities needed for their desperation flights.

To do that effectively the accuracy of bomb drops had to become more accurate, so the bombing altitude was reduced to 10,000 feet. Also, this altitude, versus 20,000 feet, was more comfortable for the crew and saved fuel since the B-24 was more efficient at this altitude. There was a report that the Japanese flak was less accurate at this altitude, but it seems doubtful that they would not soon have adjusted their calibrations for this altitude. Experience soon led to practices that reduced the danger of being hit by anti-aircraft fire. One was to loosen up the tight formations, since fighters attacking formations were almost non-existent, to allow for more maneuverability along with shorter straight runs approaching target and more evasive action just after bombs away.

We flew a few missions in June, which were more like practice to keep us in touch. We had brought a radar ship over and looked for enemy ships with this equipment on occasion but flew no real combat missions. We were told that I would probably be assigned as a copilot and the rest of the crew would be assigned to fill in positions for various crews as they needed replacements. This did not happen and we stayed together. Perhaps our check flight went well, or our squadron simply needed an intact crew.

Angaur was quite isolated and we received only scanty news, but the big news was the unconditional surrender of Germany on May 7, 1945. We wondered if the troops, planes, etc., employed in Europe would now be diverted in large part to the Pacific. Would Japan now realize that Germany's surrender would lead to events that now even more convincingly doomed her war effort? In retrospect it is amazing how naïve and ignorant we were about these events.

## Moving Closer

Angaur had become less critically positioned as U.S. forces moved westward taking, or on occasion bypassing, islands as they went. The recapture of the Philippines removed one of the 494th's most crucial targets. The 494th flew only thirteen missions in May; nevertheless, six officers and eleven enlisted men were killed or missing plus eleven were injured. Four B-24s were lost. By now we were keenly aware firsthand that casualties of the Air Corps flight crews were high. Our group had begun plans to move to a new theater of operations.

The island of Okinawa was declared "secured" on June 21, 1945, after about three months of brutal battle, the most costly of all U.S. Pacific battles. The casualties were 12,500 American lives lost and 36,000 wounded. The Japanese lost 93,000 troops and 94,000 civilian Okinawans. This island was strategic in that it was a launching pad to engage intense air raids and a platform to stage an invasion of the main islands of Japan. It was only about 350 miles south of Kyushu and about 550 miles from Honshu. We were moved to Okinawa—the home islands were definitely now in our range. Okinawa remains to this day a strategically placed U.S. air base for the far east area.

Moving the 494th required planning and time to execute. The "Ground Echelon" was moved out by transport ship starting on June 7. The "Air Echelon" of crews that were not transporting our B-24s, mostly newer crews including 42B, began movement on June 21, 1945, by transport ship USS *Alkaid*. The transport ship was anchored out far enough to clear the shallow coral reefs, and personnel and supplies were taken out by small boats.

When our crew left in a small boat to motor out to the *Alkaid* for boarding, we had all of our personal belongings on our backs in duffel bags. We left our duffel bags on the small boats and climbed up rope ladders to the deck. I watched as our bags and supplies were lifted on board from the small boats. Due to the necessary arrangement of getting things on board, quite a few of the packets being hoisted by ship board cranes got wet, even soaked, on occasion because of faulty loading and securing. My only concern at this point was our parachutes. In order to have chutes that would open properly without fail, the chute packets had to be opened and the nylon material hung to air and dry periodically. I knew that we were not likely to have such service in Okinawa, but we had to accept these conditions on this newly established "front line."

The air echelon flying the planes left Angaur on July 1 and, of course, arrived the same day. By contrast the air echelon on the *Alkaid* anchored fairly close to Ulithi Island to wait for a convoy to join going to Okinawa. A small island by Ulithi called Mog Mog was used as a recreation site for troops from various ships anchored there. We were taken in once for grilled steaks and quantities of 3.2 beer. We finally got to Okinawa July 11. We were stationed at Yontan Airfield, which had just been bulldozed and packed before our planes landed there on July 1. The Yontan area was still being polished when we got there.

The 494th went into action almost immediately upon arrival, flying missions against Japanese bases on islands north of Okinawa, Kyushu, the southernmost main island of Japan, and Shanghai, China. Dave Rogers, 494th historian, wrote: "Scarcely allowing time for the air echelon to catch its breath after arrival at Okinawa, the group was plunged into action. . . . Conducting operations against a determined enemy strongly entrenched on home soil was found to be a different story when compared to the enemy resistance the group had met over the Philippine Islands. Unprecedented losses in both personnel and aircraft were suffered by the group during its first month of operation from Okinawa." As the main islands of Japan were approached closer and closer, the Japanese defense became even more and more desperate and intense on land, sea, and air.

## Initiation

The 494th flew several missions against major airfields on Kyushu and other islands before my crew flew its first mission. It was on July 17, 1945, against the major Japanese air base of Chiang Wan at Shanghai, the first strike of our group to China, that we were initiated. Even the old hands were apprehensive because of the unknown—especially the amount and accuracy of their anti-aircraft. We were briefed early in the morning with an unusual amount of information about being captured and were given information packets in Chinese and issued Chinese money, which could to help get one to friendly natives. Such options were absent in Japan. All of this did not ease feelings.

The chaplain waved to us as we turned on to the runway of Yontan Airfield for takeoff. It was a long flight, flying loose formation all the way. Copilot Looper developed a severe headache, and I did almost all of the piloting, flying formation, and had a sore arm the next day. The lead plane was using radar to sight the target and all other planes were dropping off his release.

As we approached the targeted airfield, a wall of flak was thrown up, which was intimidating especially to new hands. Just after bombs away, one of our planes was hit and badly damaged and started to lose control and altitude. The crew bailed out, and we tried to count the number of chutes opening but the plane soon disappeared in clouds. This and a follow-up raid were very successful, claiming eighty percent hits and leaving large fires reported by a later reconnaissance flight. Our crew was now indoctrinated into the realities of a combat mission. Those who bailed out successfully on the two missions to Shanghai were either shot, interned by Japanese as POWs, or hidden by Chinese guerrillas. Their amazing stories are related in the *494th Bombardment Group (H) WW II History*.

Back on our base in Okinawa, on off hours we busied ourselves looking around our end of the island. It was a beehive of activity—continuing the building of a military base mostly designed to facilitate an air assault against the main islands of

Japan. When we had the opportunity, we scrounged pieces of lumber that were lying around docks in order to improve our tent. We usually paired up and would walk through the enlisted tent area and pick up any of our crew who wanted to join us. Our crew members had become even closer knit as we stayed to-gether longer—almost as a "family group." We mixed freely and enjoyed each other's company as vigorous, curious young men.

### A Date with the *Lonesome Lady*

No diversion relieved our tension about being posted for our next mission. There were no missions now that would not result in substantial casualties. On July 27, 1945, we were scheduled for an early flight the next day. At the early morning briefing, flight crews learned that our mission was to bomb the Japanese Imperial Navy BB *Haruna*, the remaining floating battleship of the Japanese Navy. This battleship was reported to be crippled and at anchor in Kure Harbor, Honshu, along with other capital ships. This was a moderately long mission for B-24s and one of the few that had been flown by Liberators to the main islands—the first to Honshu, I believe. Ironically, Air Force Col. Colin Kelley was posthumously awarded the Congressional Medal of Honor for having sunk the *Haruna* in the depths of the Pacific much earlier.

The rationale for bombing this target, as I understood it, was that we were to destroy one of the last symbols of strength of the Japanese Navy and presumably add to the incentive for them to surrender without the necessity of U.S. ground troop in-vasion. This was a strong incentive, given the casualties during invasions such as those of Okinawa and Iwo Jima.

We were warned that Kure Harbor, a major naval base and repair facility, referred to by some as the "Japanese Annapolis," was an amphitheater of anti-aircraft fire power from heavily armed ground installations plus many large ships in harbor. Although not discussed per se at the briefing, a maxim among Air Force pilots was that one should "never fly over an enemy battleship."

We were also briefed that "name, rank, and serial number" was no longer the only information that was authorized to be re-vealed to enemy captors. We were briefed to the effect that we (flight crews) did not know anything that the Japanese either did not already know or that would be of any military value to them. Therefore, we were told to fully cooperate in giving information to interrogators in order to possibly mitigate abuse. Also, if we had to bail out, we should attempt to get out to sea, where there was a possibility of being picked up by our navy, who would be patrolling in Dumbos (PBY flying boats) or submarines looking for survivors of downed planes. If we bailed out over land, we were to turn ourselves in, but if possible we were to avoid civilians and local police and seek out military personnel to accept our surrender. Escaping or finding sympathizers was totally out of the question.

On July 28, 1945, our flight crew got up at about 5:30 A.M., ate breakfast, and was briefed. We left for the flight line of Yontan Airfield to locate B-24 A/C 44-40680—the *Lonesome Lady;* we had admired her art but never flown her. The crew consisted of Looper, Pedersen, Ryan, Abel, Atkinson, Ellison, Long, and myself of our regular crew and a lower ball turret gunner, who was assigned to join us, named Ralph J. Neal.

We took off in the *Lonesome Lady* some time after 8:00 A.M., as ours was one of the last of the squadrons in line. There would have been six squadrons of six planes in a complete complement except that apparently only thirty-three planes were available to go on this mission. We formed a loose formation that arrived at the target area a little after noon. We were flying at the designated altitude of 10,000 feet above broken clouds. Our squadron tightened up its formation around the lead plane flown by Capt. Emil Turek. We were on his left wing in the *Lonesome Lady* and Joseph Dubinsky was piloting the *Taloa* in the number 4 position—just below and behind the lead plane. The *Lonesome Lady* was Turek's regular plane, but he had been assigned a new plane not yet named. The *Taloa* was the regular plane of Capt. Donald Marvin, whose crew was not scheduled to go on this mission because they had completed their forty combat missions, qualifying them for rotation back to the States. However, Marvin had missed one earlier mission due to an injury, so he went along in the *Taloa* as an observer in order to make up his missions to forty. Even though he was not required to do so, he insisted that he participate in as many missions as the rest of his crew.

### Damn Rough Mission

Our squadron was made up of four planes, since two of the original six had aborted, as we approached the target area. Turek spotted the *Haruna* through broken clouds, and his bombardier led us over the *Haruna*. We each released our three 2,000-pound GP (general purpose) bombs, amid a flurry of smoke bursts from exploding flak. All four of our planes were hit by flak. Our plane was hit just after we released our bombs. The *Taloa,* piloted by Joseph Dubinsky, was hit at about the same time as we were but was more severely damaged and went down very quickly. Turek's lead plane was also hit and lost a lot of fuel but was able to make it back to an intermediate location, Ie Shima, for an emergency landing. The fourth plane had minor hits and made it back to Yontan home base.

Turek wrote after the mission: "Dam rough mission!! Flak was intense & accurate. Approximately 3,000 bursts. We were in it for 35 minutes. Our plane was hit by a shell which went clear thru the left wing aft of #2. Fuel cell was punctured and we lost a lot of gas." An official report summarizing the actions of the 494th Bombardment Group stated about the squadron bombing the *Haruna:* "Throwing up the most terrific curtain of flak ever encountered by the 494th crews, the Japs scored twice sending two B-24s to destruction."

Lt. Vito Nacci, a bombardier on the lead plane of our squadron piloted by Turek, stated in his report that "A very few moments after bombs away at 1240 I, A/C 680 [*Lonesome Lady*] received a direct hit from an anti-aircraft shell which entered near the pitot [air speed] tube, appeared to pass through the pilot's position and that of the navigator, and out through the raft compartment." Sergeant Reeves flying on the same A/C confirmed this observation. Their observations were essentially correct except that the shell entered somewhat farther out to the right away from the flight deck. This or other bursts also damaged the bomb bay area (if we had not already released our bombs when the bomb bay was struck, they likely would have been detonated), and there was also some damage to the rear of the bomb bay (this information came from Abel). Although Abel took a hit from a piece of caroming flak, he was not seriously injured. No one aboard was severely injured, so far as I know, although I learned later that at least Ryan and Atkinson were limping badly.

Shortly after being hit, our plane began responding sluggishly to controls, and I radioed the squadron leader, Emil Turek, that I was hit and could not maintain my formation position. I had hoped to head out to sea before ordering bail-out. However, our plane was severely damaged in several areas. Fire broke out, and I began losing more control. The B-24 controls were partly hydraulic and we obviously had a ruptured line. Ellison left the flight deck to inspect damage and came back soaked in hydraulic fluid.

In his report Lieutenant Nacci further stated that "At 1304 I four parachutes were seen to leave the A/C (680) and open. The A/C did not appear to be burning, went into a vertical dive into undercast, and was not seen again." Our plane was burning but apparently in such a way as to not create much smoke at that time. We were losing altitude but were not yet in a "vertical dive." I do not recall thinking that as much as twenty minutes passed, as would be indicated by Lieutenant Nacci's report, but some time after being hit, Engineer Buford Ellison reported that there was serious damage and that the fire was spreading and appeared to be a serious threat. Also, by this time I had lost almost all control of the plane, and we were losing altitude faster, so I ordered bail-out. The intercom was knocked out and it was necessary to relay the bail-out command by two men, one to the rear of the ship and one to the nose—I believe Ellison and Atkinson relayed the command. The tail gunner, Bill Abel, had heard the bail-out bell and opened the rear hatch when Ellison and Atkinson appeared there along with Neal. According to Abel, after some hesitation about who should lead the way, Atkinson shouted in effect that "we have to get out fast" and told Bill to go ahead. The others obviously followed.

Our navigator, Roy Pedersen, because of his position on the flight deck, was the first to reach the bomb bay doors through which we were to jump. He came back to my position and reported that the doors were stuck closed. The doors were designed so that they could be kicked out in an emergency, so I ordered that he do so. Roy was a stout, capable, determined person and could easily handle this emergency procedure.

I was consumed with trying to cope with the fractured and unresponsive *Lonesome Lady* as we were by then losing altitude rapidly, but shortly after Pedersen left I did manage to see that everyone had apparently cleared the flight deck and entrance to the bomb bay. I motioned to Copilot Durden Looper, and he left to bail out. I do know that the flight deck and bomb bay were clear of people when I scrambled through on my hands and knees as the *Lonesome Lady* began gyrating. I dived out head first and saw the ground coming up fast, so I pulled my rip cord immediately instead of waiting, as I had planned in order to avoid being a hanging target. The shock of the chute opening and popping me tight in the harness and the shock of hitting the ground seemed only seconds apart. An eyewitness, Mr. Taniyama, from the village of Amakane, close to the crash sight of the *Lonesome Lady* reported to Mr. Mori in 1995 that this "crippled bomber flew from the west around 1300 on July 28, 1945 . . . the right inner propeller of the plane was not moving. The plane circled the sky before plunging to the ground head down."

The report of Lieutenant Nacci and my recollection seem to be consistent except for the fire and vertical dive. I do not know who were in the four chutes reported by Lieutenant Nacci. Looper and I went out later, and we were undoubtedly missed in the sighting. Two or three chutes were not accounted for in the sightings, which is not unexpected given the circumstances. I saw Looper, Ryan, Atkinson, Ellison, Long, and Neal alive in a prison. I know almost certainly that Troy Pedersen got out. He may have gotten entangled with the bomb bay doors as they ripped off, or his chute may have been fouled and failed in some way (recall the earlier observation that our chutes may have gotten soaked while loading on the troop ship *Alkaid*), but I am convinced that he did not go down with the *Lonesome Lady* as the Japanese records reflect. (The above paragraph was written before I received information from Mr. Mori about Roy's fate.)

## POW

I landed in an open spot in an isolated pine forest, gathered and hid my chute, and decided to discard the ammunition to my .45 automatic pistol so that the Japanese could not have it. Within perhaps ten to fifteen minutes I spotted a farmer (identified later by Mr. Mori as Mr. Seiichi Tamai) walking along a path through the forest where I came down. This single man was my best bet, I decided, to get taken safely to the military. When I stepped out in front of him on the path it startled this fellow so much that he was visibly shaken. I tried to convey to him that I wanted him to take me to the military. My .45 automatic sidearm was the major cause of his alarm; he did not know that I had no ammunition. I finally pointed down the path in the direction he had come from and followed him.

He led me to a local, one-room police station in a nearby village. Looper was brought into the same station a short time later. There was much excitement in this small station by the few police and the citizenry outside, especially whenever I reached for my pistol to turn it in. They were armed only with clubs and sticks; there was one person standing in the doorway with a pitchfork as if guarding our escape. I finally did turn in my pistol by placing it on a table, walking away, and sitting down by Looper. The police then demanded that we empty our pockets of everything.

We were not allowed to talk with one another or to treat our cuts and bruises with our pocket first aid kits—Looper had a rather nasty-looking bruise on one of his legs. We were both excessively thirsty from our ordeal and asked for (signaled for) and were given water. Soon we were blindfolded and had our hands tied behind our backs and were walked to a larger village close by. Apparently, there were quite a few villagers who joined in along the way and followed the entourage with some harassment.

When we arrived, we were sat on the ground, presumably in the town square, and kept there into the night. We were hit and pinched, but mostly by women, I think. This experience was very similar to that of a B-29 crew whose plane went down in the Sea of Japan August 8, 1945. They survived in a life raft until drifting to a Japanese fishing village where they were captured and put on display until the military arrived and saved them. The book *Courage Beyond the Blindfold* by the bombardier Walter Ross gives some details of their treatment. Also see below regarding this crew's encounter with Neal from the *Lonesome Lady* and Brissette from the *Ticonderoga* aircraft carrier. Again, our treatment while on display was very similar to that described in the book *Accused American War Criminal* by Fiske Hanley II, a B-29 engineer shot down while laying mines in the strait between Kyushu and Honshu. He vividly described the two-handed pinch that women inflicted with considerable pain.

The next morning a small military truck arrived with an officer and several armed guards who took charge of Looper and me for transport. I presumed that we were going to a military base. I thought that we had been very fortunate up to this point to have survived a massive barrage of exploding anti-aircraft shells, bailed out from an out of control plane, been captured by civilians, and held by local police (especially considering the experience of the crew of the *Taloa*).

For the journey we were again blindfolded and tied, hands behind our backs. The truck travel was slow and after a short trip we were transferred to a train; the total trip, including delays, took perhaps a little over a half day. We arrived at what I perceived to be a large city, judging from the noise and traffic. We could not see much more than a bit of daylight from under our blindfolds and could not have read Japanese signs even if we could have seen them.

I now know that the city was Hiroshima. We were taken directly to a building where we were untied and blindfolds removed, and then put in a fairly large cell on the first floor. I was elated to see that all of the remainder of our crew were there in that cell except for Bill Abel and Roy Pedersen. Also, I recognized Baumgartner from the *Taloa*. There were several other prisoners present, including two U. S. Navy men. I was not surprised that most of our crew was gathered together at one point, but I was surprised that they put us together. I hoped that Pedersen and Abel were in similar locations after surviving bail-out and capture; in fact I was somewhat optimistic about them at this point.

Prisoners were required to sit on the floor with backs against the wall; standing or moving about would bring a strong rebuke. We spent the night stretched out on the bare floor. We were watched constantly by guards in the continuously lighted cell and were not allowed to talk or signal to each other. We were allowed to periodically use the single bucket provided as the toilet called the honey bucket or "benjo." Looper and I sat together, having arrived last, against one wall looking right across at our other crew members. All of the crew appeared bedraggled, but I detected no apparent serious physical injury. Ryan limped badly when he walked to urinate in the honey bucket. Long had a bandage around his head but appeared alert. I'm sure we all had similar thoughts: where were Pedersen and Abel, and what are the Japanese going to do with us?

At one time, in retrospect, I had thought that the prison where we were taken was Hiroshima Castle. Later, judging from reports of DeWalt, Manoff, and others, the location was later established as having been the Chugoku Military Police Headquarters, close to the grounds of the Hiroshima Castle, in the Motomachi district of Hiroshima. My crew could have been moved after I left, but the evidence indicates that they were in the Chugoku Military Police Headquarters location on August 6. This building is reported to have been about 1,320 feet from the epicenter of the explosion of the atomic bomb.

The day after arriving in Hiroshima, I was taken out and interrogated by a Japanese officer in a sparsely furnished room on the second floor, so I knew that the building had at least two floors. He was assisted by an interpreter who spoke fairly good English. I could see one tall building out the window of this office. Also, I had developed diarrhea (perhaps from the village water) and was hastily blindfolded and taken out of the building to a public toilet close by during an intermission in the interrogation. While in the small toilet building, my blindfold was removed, and I was able to get a glimpse of a bridge across a small river through the open entry and exit doorways.

The interrogating officer did not impress me as a trained interrogator. He started friendly, offered me a cigarette, and gradually escalated his demeanor toward hostility, and when he became frustrated would slap my hands, arms, or head with a kind of swagger stick, but he was not excessively abusive. One of the key questions that he asked me followed his statement that "this large city" (which he did not name) had not been bombed—he wanted to know why it had been spared. This statement and the few glimpses that I got of the city, along with the other circumstances, caused me, after reflection at a later time, to believe that the city was Hiroshima. After about two hours with an intermission (as mentioned above for a toilet break), my interrogator told me that he knew that I was not telling him the truth (which I was) in response to questions about rather routine military operations (mostly about my own movements across the Pacific to Okinawa and about military buildup about which I was ignorant of any substantial facts) and therefore would be taken to an interrogation center.

### Interrogation Center

The next morning, when I was taken out of our cell away from my crew and blindfolded and tied for the trip, I felt a little sorry for myself. I was joined with the two American naval personnel and taken to a train station. The train trip took most of two days with many delays and a layover one night in a bare room in a place that I later learned was in the city of Osaka. When we were taken out to board the train, a hostile crowd had gathered and called for us to be killed, but we were only aware of some sort of disturbance about our presence.

We were taken to what was obviously a military base and put in separate cells in what appeared to be a brig for the base, but no other prisoners were in this fairly small building. The cell had wooden bars, no window, and a dim light hanging from the ceiling that burned through the night. There was nothing else in the cell except one threadbare blanket. We were watched constantly by a guard for our three cells through the wooden bars that looked out over a hallway and were allowed to stand only to use the "honey bucket" or be taken out for interrogation. We were never allowed to talk to our mates in the adjoining cells. Our daily ration consisted of one rice ball (*onigiri*) about the size of a small softball and water (*mizu*). No baths were provided. I learned later that the location where I had been held was the Imperial General Headquarters located in Tokyo.

There were many visitors who came by to look at the bedraggled enemy soldiers. From the looks of some who came to look at us and stared at us for what seemed like an hour, I was glad to be protected by the wooden bars. The guards were all young and seemed to show us off, but they were never menacing themselves. They had two shifts and ate their meals while standing guard.

I was interrogated by a pair of officers each day for two or three days. The questioning always started somewhat friendly and intensified as it progressed and ended with threats of punishment for lying.

About the fourth day I was rushed out of my solitary cell and questioned intensively about a new powerful bomb. There were trick questions and threats. One compelling threat that followed immediately after this interrogation session was having a very large Japanese soldier come by my cell and stand right in front of my bars and, while looking at me, draw a sword and display it menacingly. I was then marched out blindfolded in front of some troops, pushed down on my knees, and my head pushed down with all the indications of being beheaded. After a few minutes of commands or some sort of oration shouted at the troops while I was in this position, I was jerked up and rather roughly led back to my cell. Having been blindfolded, I can only conjecture from noises, commands, sounds, etc. about the troops and other actions that might have been taking place. It is interesting to note that Lieutenant Hanley, a B-29 POW, in his book *Accused War Criminal* described a very similar experience while being held at the Kempei Tai Headquarters in Tokyo. It was a very traumatic experience, but I was not terrified—why, I do not know.

Of course, I knew nothing of real importance and the interrogators probably knew that I knew nothing. But they were desperate, with a growing resentment, and had become even more vengeful. Strangely, I was not questioned after this incident. I had always been truthful and straightforward in the interrogations, and I tried not to behave in an arrogant manner and show my feelings. I believe that this helped me. Also, I believe that they were sensing that the end was near and at least some realized that it was in their best interest to not have blood on their hands. The fact that my guards were quite young, rather than hardened old-line soldiers, already with blood on their hands, may have been part of the reason for being spared the frustrated vengeance which was common.

### Strange Music

Some days later, about midmorning, music came over the camp PA system that had previously been used only for what I presumed were verbal messages or commands. The music sounded like funeral dirges to me. I was very apprehensive; my thought was that the emperor's palace had been bombed and he had been killed and that would certainly bring retribution. After the music stopped about midday, there was a strange silence where there had always been various levels of noise in the background. Everyone that I could see (a few guards) stood at attention and listened to a person talking in a serious modulated tone which was very subdued compared to the usual screeching commands. Later I learned that the music must have been the Japanese national anthem, the "Kimagayo." The voice must have been that of a recording of Emperor Hirohito reading his famous rescript on August 15, 1945, saying, in his obtuse way, that Japan had been defeated—the war was over. To quote a partial translation: "However, it is according to the dictate of time and fate that we have resolved to pave the way for a grand peace for all the generations to come by enduring the unendurable and suffering what is insufferable." The Japanese people had never before heard the voice of their emperor/God.

There was a somber mood among the guards for the rest of the day. The next day one of the guards, who was quite young but had been very authoritative and domineering, came to my cell and smiled. Some dried fish was brought with my daily rice ball and this guard who spoke some English greeted me solicitously, asking such questions as "Are you well? How are your parents? Are they old? Are they well cared for?" Then he said, "We will take you to a better place and soon you may be reunited with your parents." Of course, my mind was racing and afraid to believe what everything indicated.

My fate was in contrast to other reports of American POWs being killed, often by being beheaded, rather than being repatriated after hearing that Japan had surrendered. In the book *Fall of Japan* by William Craig, it is reported that at "Fukuoka one hundred miles north of the burning remains of Nagasaki" at the Western Army District Headquarters on August 11, 1945, that—with prolonged flourish and brutality—eight POWs from downed B-29s were individually tormented and beheaded. Four days later after the emperor's rescript was broadcast, the remaining fliers there were to be executed with orders from the officer in charge that "the execution will be kept secret." Craig added that one vital reason impelled the Japanese to act against the remaining B-29 crew members in detention at the headquarters: "They knew too much. They could testify. . ." All of the POWs were reported to have been taken to a secluded spot and, with onlookers such as an officer's girlfriend, were individually hacked to pieces with swords in an orgy of death. Craig also wrote that "Shortly after the Emperor broadcast the news of defeat, over fifty airmen there [Osaka] were beheaded by vengeful Japanese soldiers."

The next day I was taken on a relatively short trip via a charcoal-burning truck through the outskirts of the large city to a designated POW camp, which was on the small dredged island of Omori in Tokyo-Yokohama Bay. I learned later that this camp had been marked POW only in the last few days. There I had no blindfold and was free to walk about the camp. I met a mixed group of POWs, new arrivals like me, and old hands including Australians, British, Canadian, Italian, New Zealanders as well as Americans who had been taken as POWs from the Philippines, Singapore, other Asian cities, and navy submarine and surface ships. The new arrivals were all from B-29, B24, navy and other aircraft who had gone down over or near Japan. The notorious Col. "Pappy" Boyington of the "Black Sheep Squadron" and Comdr. Richard O'Kane from the submarine *Tang* were there. Both had been awarded the Congressional Medal of Honor, but the announcement of this honor had been withheld until after the war to avoid possible reprisal to them. Also at the camp were Robert Martindale and Fiske Hanley, whose books are quoted in this work.

There had been no source of news available to the POWs, but by this time it was clear that the Japanese were capitulating in some manner. When U.S. warships were spotted sailing into Tokyo Bay, there was no doubt.

We were given minimal but improved rations (a few vegetables with rice balls), improved quarters (a thin grass mat on a wooden shelf and a threadbare blanket), and medical care (iodine and aspirin). All of the POWs were thin, but the B-29 crews who had been recently brought in from various locations where they had been held in strategic military locations in and around Tokyo were in various stages of emaciation and shock from the maltreatment they had received. The treatment of B-29 crews was dramatically portrayed by Jim Lehrer in his recent novel *The Special*

*Prisoner* and by Fiske Hanley in *Accused American War Criminal.* In fact, B-29 airmen had not been considered POWs but instead were classed as Japanese federal prisoners being held for murder for bombing civilian locations; inhumane treatment of them was thus encouraged. (It should be noted that the Japanese are generally credited for being the first country to bomb civilian populations when they bombed China in the 1930s.)

The guards and other Japanese now kept out of sight as much as possible, and on August 26 (as best I can remember) we woke up to find that most of the Japanese guards had vanished in the night from the island. Later that day, American transport planes dropped supplies to us by parachute including toothpaste, toothbrushes, razors, soap, and various packages of rations, candy, coffee, and cigarettes. The candy came down in an orange-colored chute and landed in the notorious honey pit but was recovered, and I cut a piece of that chute as a souvenir. The mood was ecstatic—in fact, a bit wild. Colonel Boyington, a rather compulsive fellow, overdosed on caffeine from the coffee, and several of us took turns sitting up and talking with him the night through. Some of the old-hand Australians swam ashore with cigarettes, soap, and candy wrapped in condoms (source unknown to me). They reported on return great success in bartering their supplies to very friendly women. These old hands had been very ingenious in getting extra food from docks where they unloaded supplies even under the close surveillance of the guards and thus had the energy for such escapades. The POWs from B-29 crews were beyond thoughts of bold forays and women.

My bunk, a place on a shelf four feet above ground, was right above a B-29 crewman who had been shot down over Tokyo. He had been kept in Tokyo, where he was starved and brutalized before being brought to Omori. He called me "Tarzan" because I was strong enough to jump down from my bunk shelf. Since he could not walk without assistance, he asked me to take him to a religious service that a Catholic chaplain on Omori had organized. His sermon was, in effect, to not forget our war experiences when we got home but to not let memories of harsh treatment be an excuse for not contributing to society. Leading a full, productive life would be much more satisfying. This advice stuck in my memory. At the time I was young and vigorous and knew that I had the fortitude to do this, but then I was thinking of myself and did not know what had happened to my crew.

## Liberated

Before the Japanese capitulated, President Truman had called a meeting to consider the Japanese response to the "Potsdam Declaration" of conditions of surrender; it was a conditional response requesting that the emperor retain his sovereignty. Present were James Forrestal, secretary of the navy; Adm. William Leahy; Henry Stimson, secretary of war; and James Byrnes, secretary of state. They all agreed that the emperor should remain in order to help calm the transition. According to Craig in his book *The Fall of Japan,* while waiting for a response from Japan this group received an urgent message from Gen. George Marshall urging that allied POWs be released immediately and be moved to a spot where they could receive immediate medical attention. His expression of concern may have been a factor in the navy sending a preemptive rescue mission to Omori which was sitting in the bay close by. (It is not clear to me why the venerable General Marshall was not included more in the considerations of dropping the atomic bombs and conditions of the peace terms with Japan.)

On August 28, Commander Harold Stassen, former governor of Minnesota, came into our view from Omori with a small flotilla of landing craft manned by marines and with cameras mounted up front. Commander Stassen and Commander Roger Simpson were in charge of plans to liberate POWs. Omori was the closest camp to their flotilla, and they requested permission to liberate the POWS there. Adm. William Halsey is reported to have replied to their request to liberate Omori as the first camp: "These are our boys, go get them." The crafts had to avoid ramming into some who had jumped in the water to swim out to meet this welcome party. Craig wrote in *The Fall of Japan* that "prisoners from Omori ran out to the shoreline to greet members of the Fourth Marine Regiment. As landing barges moved toward shore, battle hardened Marines saw emaciated Americans wading out into the surf, crying hysterically, sobbing out inarticulate greetings. As they approached closer, the men in the boats wept too."

Finally, the marines managed to land among a jubilant group who cooperatively scrambled on board and were spirited away to various U.S. ships which had moved into the bay. A picture of the POWs crowded together in a cheering throng greeting the first landing craft was widely circulated. I can be spotted in the picture with only my head pushing through the crowd.

A book published in 1998 entitled *Hap's War* describes the experiences of Capt. Ray "Hap" Halloran, the navigator on a B-29 shot down on January 27, 1945, including his transfer to Omori, the conditions, and his experiences there. Also, the book *The 13th Mission* by Robert Martindale, subtitled *Prisoners of the Notorious Omori Prison in Tokyo,* describes in some detail life of POWs at Omori. These books have aerial and other photos of Omori.

I was first taken to a destroyer and then transferred to the cruiser USS *Reeves*. Hot showers to scrub away dirt, as well as fleas and lice, and then clean clothes were a treat.

All the navy had to offer us were their NCO shipboard clothes, which we were glad to get. We feasted on ham, ice cream, etc. only to our regret. Some of the men from B-29 crews were so emaciated from near starvation that they could eat only a few bites. For most of us this debilitation soon passed. A navy hammock felt so good I just lay there for about ten hours.

Commander Stassen had liberated us "illegally" since no peace agreement had been signed and U.S. forces were under orders to not go ashore in Japan. We waited in Tokyo Bay on naval ships for a few days until September 7, when the formal peace agreement was signed aboard the USS *Missouri*, which was in our view from on the *Reeves*. We, of course, did not know exactly what was happening, but we easily guessed that something important had happened when 400 B-29s and 1,500 carrier planes conducted a flyover. We were impressed but the point, we assumed, was to impress the vanquished that we were now in full control. After the signing we were put on board a transport-type landing craft and shuttled to a close by port in Yokohama. We were picked up there by U.S. Army 6x6 trucks and transported to Atsugi Airport, where U.S. troops had first landed in Japan. Along the way many Japanese stood by the road waving and smiling. We were then ushered onto a Douglas C-54 transport plane that flew us to Okinawa, landing at my old base airfield of Yontan.

Upon arriving at Okinawa I immediately made my way to the 494th Bombardment Group area—my old outfit. I was greeted with incredulous stares and second takes. First, I was wearing U. S. Navy seaman's clothes (all that the navy had to give me) and, second, I was a ghost. I literally interrupted an officer who had been laboring over composing a letter to my parents with condolences and stating what little information that he had. The *Lonesome Lady* had last been seen in a nose dive, only four parachutes had been spotted, and the report of Lieutenant Nacci indicated that the anti-aircraft shell had pierced the pilot compartment.

Shortly after my arrival there, Bill Abel showed up also in Navy attire. We shook hands and hugged and shook hands and hugged—we continued this routine spontaneously until we departed. We exchanged stories and started looking for our buddies to show up. We finally had to report to our ships, but we were in good spirits.

Bill told me that he lost intercom connection when we were hit. He knew that we were severely damaged, and when he heard the "bail out" bell he left his tail gunner's turret and opened the rear emergency hatch and bailed out as indicated above. After his chute popped open, he looked for our plane, did not see it, and then looked down at some farmers below who were moving toward where he was headed for a landing. He came down in a wooded area and his chute caught on a large tree. He cut himself loose, dropped to the ground, hid his orange "Mae West" vest, and ran uphill toward a mountainous area he had seen joining the wooded area where he had come down. The Japanese farmers trailing him went downhill first and then spread out uphill toward the mountain, "beating the bushes." He crawled into a hollow tree, covered the entrance with debris, and stayed there until the search party passed by him going up and then down the mountain. He came out at night and was able to stay undetected for nine days. He could find almost nothing to eat, so he knew that he had to turn himself in.

His hiding place was elevated so that he could see a train station in a nearby town where he had noted that a passenger train pulled out early each morning. During the night he slipped into the station and boarded this train and was undetected until passengers started boarding. When he saw people come into the car, he sat up in a seat like a passenger and pulled his cap over his face. His beard had grown out and his flight suit was dirty and torn. Strangely, the passengers walked right past, ignoring or apparently avoiding him because of his dirty appearance. As the train car filled, passengers sat in rows next to him. A boy, perhaps fourteen or fifteen years old, sat beside him and soon began to notice his unusual appearance and clothes, so he leaned down to peer under his cap. Startled, this boy called "He has blue eyes" (exactly what the boy said is conjecture) and other passengers began to shout "American, American!" Bill had entered the train expecting that a military person would be among the passengers, and just as the shouts attracted everyone's attention, a military man in a white naval uniform entered the car. Bill jumped up and grabbed this person, turning himself in. (Japanese records reflect that this naval officer captured Sergeant Abel.) He was held at a prison with a number of oriental appearing prisoners and one other American, a navy flier shot down over Kure Harbor. I do not know the details, but at various times he was beaten and suffered kidney damage from being kicked. After the emperor announced that Japan had surrendered, he was told that he would be taken to an "American" prison. This place was Ofuna POW Camp, which was close to Yokohama—a place where "Pappy" Boyington had been held earlier. Mr. Mori reported from an interview in 1996 with an eighty-one-year-old but clear-minded man, Mr. Akitaka Fujita, who had been a high-ranking military officer, that Bill Abel was arrested by military police in Kure.

## Waiting . . . Hoping

From Okinawa, I was taken to the Philippines with other former POWs and given physicals. After a few days we shipped to San Francisco on the hospital ship USS *Benevolence*. We were met at the gang plank by former Omori POW Fiske Hanley, a number of brass, and some very excited relatives. As soon as we arrived I called Carolyn and my parents. We were bused to the attractive Presidio where we were given an extensive physical at Letterman Military Hospital. We were awarded the Purple Heart and a few more medals and in my case a promotion to first lieutenant. Then, after a few days, I was given leave to go home, recuperate, and be released from duty effective February 23, 1946.

I was given a document from the Adjutant General, War Department, dated October 4, 1945, which stated, in part, that "personnel who have . . . been imprisoned or interned by the enemy . . . and have been released . . . are permitted to disclose, relate or publish the details of their own experiences, provided, however, that no information will be divulged concerning" such things as "secret intelligence" and "negotiations conducted on high government or military level." I did not believe that any restriction was placed on me concerning revealing my POW experience to any source, but at the time this just seemed another proliferation of military paperwork. No military source sought any information from me concerning my POW experience except routine documentation of dates, etc.

It was not until I had returned home that I had access to written accounts and pictures of Hiroshima. In the absence of any word whatsoever about the rest of my crew, I began to fit the pieces of information and my recollection together. I became convinced that the remainder of my crew had been held in Hiroshima and were casualties of the atomic bomb. I wrote letters to the War Department, most of which were acknowledged but usually only perfunctorily.

Unfortunately, I did not keep copies of any of this correspondence. However, I recently uncovered an undated outline draft of a letter that I wrote in response to an acknowledgment of one of my letters from the War Department and asking for more information. This handwritten draft had apparently been inadvertently stuffed in a military order, filed away, and forgotten until I recently went through every military document that I had to confirm some dates of when I was stationed at various places. This draft stated, in part, that "I believe the men of my crew [who were named above] were interned in the M P Hdqrs . . . I believe the city to have been Hiroshima." I went on to give all the details that I knew about the prison building and interrogation questions such as "why has this city not been bombed," etc. to document the basis for my concluding that the city was Hiroshima.

## Official Responses

An internal message of the General Headquarters, U. S. Army Forces, Pacific, Adjutant General's Office, dated October 9, 1945, states "Investigation reveals that 2nd Lt [sic] Ralph J Neal, one Norman Roland Brisset [sic], one Blankbek [apparently a B-29 crew member shot down over Kyushu], and 17 other American airmen (names unknown) were being held in Hiroshima at time of atomic bombing. All except Neal and Brisset [sic] killed instantly. These died 19th August as result of wounds sustained in bombing . . . Further attempts being made to secure names of other 17 casualties."

Mr. Gary DeWalt, producer/director of the documentary film *Genbaku Shi* (killed by the atomic bomb), wrote the following summary of his research findings:

> The occupation forces of the U.S. Army were provided a list of American POW [Hiroshima atomic] bomb victims. This list was prepared by members of the Japanese military. They identified 20 POW bomb victims. Nine of those identified had actually been killed in medical experiments or had been executed by the Japanese prior to the dropping of the atomic bomb on Hiroshima. An attempt was made to disguise the victims of these atrocities by naming them as bomb victims. The documentary evidence in support of this finding is voluminous.
>
> Copies of microfilm reports made by the Japanese to the U.S. military occupying force, later uncovered by Mr. Mori, confirm the above although the exact number of American POWs is still in question.

Records of which I am aware reflect that notices of missing in action and then of death were given to the next of kin of Roy Pedersen and the six crew members of the *Lonesome Lady* that I personally saw in a prison cell on August 30 and 31, 1945. Some of these notices and related incidents are summarized below.

## Roy Pedersen

A message from the War Department to Roy's parents received in April 1945 was summarized by Mrs. Roy Pedersen, Sr.

as follows: "Lt. Roy S. Pedersen was killed in action July 28th over Kyushu." The designation of Kyushu was obviously an error—it should have stated Honshu. There was no other information and the family was asked not to write since any other information that became available would be sent to them. National Archives records state that "Lt. Roy M. [*sic*] Pedersen, Jr., the navigator of the plane [identified as the *Lonesome Lady*] died either when an anti-aircraft shell passed through the plane near his station or in the crash" of the *Lonesome Lady*. I know that he was not killed by an anti-aircraft shell. I know almost certainly that he left the plane and that this official statement is not accurate. It is well established that the Japanese consistently violated established Geneva Treaty procedures for treating POWs and often tried to cover this fact up by altering records of place and cause of death. His remains along with dog tags were found in 1947 and were recovered in April 1949 and returned to his family for burial in Atlantic Cemetery, Atlantic, Iowa.

After I had written the above, Mr. Shigeaki Mori made contact with me. We exchanged several letters before I asked him if he had any information about the documentation and specifics of the discovery of Roy's remains. He then interviewed several sources of eyewitnesses and found local documents in order to obtain more information about the discovery of his remains. His efforts, mainly in the area where the *Lonesome Lady* crashed, were extensive, first yielding several sources of information that were inconsistent, but persisting until we were both satisfied that he had come up with a true account in all essential details. The account follows.

An eyewitness reported in 1995 that in 1945 he saw "five parachutes from the crippled airplane but one did not open and hit the ground. The Japanese Military Police searched the area for about one week but no U.S. soldier was discovered." In 1997 a police report from the small village of Takamori, which was closest to the crash site, was discovered. The translated title of the report is *Finding of a U.S. Soldier's Remains and its Move*. Mr. Mori's handwritten translation of the report read: "His remains were found around 9:00 A.M. on September 29, 1947. A farmer Ryuji Morishita found them first in a wood, then a woodcutter, Fusaichi Kawamura. A Japanese doctor, Chikao Makibayashi, police officers and a British doctor arrived at the site later. The remains were acknowledged as Lt. Roy Pedersen by the identification tags (dog tags), parachute pack and harness, pistol and ammunition, watch and other items that he had carried with him were found in the area."

Mr. Mori further translated and summarized the doctor's report as follows: "The bones were much larger than those of Japanese and compound fractures of all large bones meant that he died from excessive bleeding by a visceral cleft. It seemed that he was hardly struck on the ground [he struck the ground hard]." The report included a sketch of the bones recovered.

I am grateful for Mr. Mori's untiring efforts to solve this mystery for several reasons. One is simply that of seeking the truth. Of much relief to me is that it put to rest the gnawing thought I had harbored that Roy was captured, killed by his captors, and then his remains were placed at the crash site. That he died instantly is more humane. Also it confirms that I did not leave Roy in the plane and had actually bailed out last as I thought.

### Durden Looper

Mrs. Ruth Looper, wife of Durden, was informed by letter dated February 19, 1946, from the adjutant general, U.S. War Department, that "It has now been officially established from reports received in the War Department that he was killed in action on August 6, 1945, while a prisoner of war at Hiroshima, Japan." Then on February 28, 1946, Mrs. Looper wrote the Adjutant General requesting information about the details surrounding his death. The adjutant general replied in a letter dated April 10, 1946, that "Information available in the War Department reveals that Lieutenant Looper was killed during the atomic bombing of Hiroshima . . . It is believed that your husband was interned at the Chugoku Military Police Building and that his death occurred there during the Atomic bomb raid on Hiroshima." The general explained that these statements were based on "Details contained in a statement made by Second Lieutenant Thomas C. Cartwright . . ." This statement is obviously the letter that I wrote during the fall of 1945 that is referred to above.

### Jim Ryan

A telegram from the U.S. War Department dated February 25, 1946, as summarized by Jim's brother Francis Ryan, reported Jim's death to his parents. A letter from the U.S. Adjutant General of the Army, dated August 28, 1947, in reply to a specific request from Jim's parents routed through channels, established Jim's presence in Hiroshima through my report. His letter then stated that "Hiroshima was destroyed as the result of atomic bombing on August 6 1945 and Lieutenant Ryan lost his life during this action. At the time the *Lonesome Lady* was shot down."

Francis Ryan was a marine stationed on Saipan and was being trained for an invasion of Kyushu in November 1945 where kamikaze pilots were being concentrated with hoarded fighter planes and civilians were being trained to fight and indoctrinated with "bushido" or "honor before death." He has reflected in a letter to me that dropping the atomic bomb on Hiroshima killed his brother but saved his life, because he felt sure that the first wave of Marines invading Japan would be killed to the man. The fact that there was an order from the Japanese Supreme Council for the Direction of the War that every POW was to be treated in a "shobun" manner (a typically indirect Japanese way of delivering an order to execute) if the allied forces attempted to invade any of Japan's home islands, compounds the irony of the fate of these brothers. (See the book *Shobun* by Michael Goodwin.)

### Ralph Neal

The following account was excerpted or quoted from *Day One, Before Hiroshima and After* by Peter Wyden and other sources. Neal was personally seen on August 17 by ten U.S. B-29 crewmen who were shot down August 8, 1945, ditched off the coast of Japan, spent a week on a life raft, and then were picked up by a Japanese fishing boat. They were tied hand and legs, blindfolded, and taken to a place identified as East Drill Field, which is in the vicinity of Hiroshima. They were laid on the ground, kicked, and abused. The hostility of the crowd escalated to the point that the fishermen who had captured them were preparing a chopping block for beheading them. At that time, Military Police Lieutenant Nobuichi Fukui, who had been assigned to take charge of the prisoners, first appeared. He had been to the U.S., had spent some time at Dartmouth, spoke English well, and was sympathetic. Upon seeing the scene he ordered that the American prisoners be loaded on a truck to take them to the Port of Ujina, where he thought they would be safer. He had to shout at the mob that he was the responsible authority before they would let him leave. "In front of Hiroshima Station [in the middle of Hiroshima], Fukui ordered the truck stopped and the blindfolds removed. 'Look what you have done!' he shouted. 'One bomb! One bomb!'" The Americans, who had not known where they were or about the atomic bomb, "sat dumbfounded in their truck as they drove through the city" and the only sound was Fukui, who kept yelling, "'One bomb! One bomb! One bomb!' On the edge of town the truck stopped and two more American POWs were loaded aboard."

They were Ralph Neal from the *Lonesome Lady* crew and naval aviator Norman Brissette, whose Curtis Helldiver from the Aircraft Carrier USS *Ticonderoga* was also shot down July 28 in Kure Harbor. "They were in appalling condition and suffering from much pain and nausea. I'll never forget the horrible green stuff that came out of their mouths and ears" recalled the B-29 radio operator. He further said that "The two ailing men were able to relate that they had been among several groups of American fliers held in Hiroshima on August 6. They remembered an explosion, fires, total hysteria, and confusion among the Japanese, and how they saved themselves by diving into a cesspool and remaining there until the fire abated." They had never heard of an atomic bomb, and no one on the truck knew that Brissette and Neal's symptoms signified that they were fatally ill from radiation poisoning. Brissette and Neal had been severely beaten, and the B-29 crew, who had also been beaten, assumed that their illness was due to this treatment. That night, confined in the cells of a Japanese military camp in Ujina, the two dying men were screaming in pain. The agony of the dying men continued through the night. Levine, one of the B-29 crew, recalled that "They were begging us to please shoot them and end it all. And finally they died before daylight [on August 19]." Neal and Brissette were the only Americans in Hiroshima on August 6, 1945, who were known, as documented by

U.S. eyewitness sources, to have lived past the immediate effects of the atomic blast and firestorm.

"Although the deaths of Americans at Hiroshima soon became known to General Groves (Brig. General Leslie Groves, Commander of the Manhattan Project) and the War Department, the United States government never informed the families of these men that the cause of their death had been an American A-bomb."

(After the above was written about Ralph Neal, the bombardier of the B-29 crew cited above, Lt. Walter Ross, published a book entitled *Courage Beyond The Blindfold*, which corroborated this account except for minor details).

### Hugh Atkinson

A passage from the book *The Jesuits,* which is about a Catholic religious order, quotes Father Pedro Arrupe, who was based in a village at the edge of Hiroshima in 1945 (page 351): Father Arrupe ". . . was one of the few westerners who witnessed the clubbing to death of an American flyer at Hiroshima the morning after 'Little Boy' was dropped. The American, a survivor from a B-29 [B-24] called *Lonesome Lady* was described by one onlooker as 'the handsomest boy I ever saw,' with 'blond hair, green eyes, white wax-like skin, a big body, and very strong looking like a lion.' The Japanese tied him to a pole on Aioi Bridge [the sighting target of Bombardier Ferebee on the *Enola Gay*] with a note pinned on him. It said, 'Beat this American Soldier Before You Pass.' . . . the Hiroshimans passing by clubbed and stoned the boy . . . to death."

Other sources essentially confirm this scene. According to several Japanese witnesses, one American was seen crawling out from under the rubble of the Chugoku Military Headquarters; he was caught by civilians, tied to the bridge post, and "beaten to death and after death." One source has identified him by name.

In a letter from Mr. Mori to me in 1996, an alternative account of Hugh Atkinson's death was proposed based on an interview by Mr. Mori in 1996 of an eyewitness. The account follows:

Sgt. Atkinson was injured in one of the legs when he was captured. After he was treated he was taken to Chugoku Military

Headquarter. In the headquarter he was fed better than the other POWs. He was given food for Japanese Military officers. When the bomb was dropped on Aug. 6, 1945, Sgt. Atkinson was with the Japanese Military polices inside the totally destroyed building. Sgt. Kuzuo Kuramoto, a Japanese military police found them and attempted to assist Sgt. Atkinson on his shoulder to a concrete building in Nekoyacho where approximately 500 MPs were stationed. However Sgt. Kuramoto himself became extremely ill around the east end of Aioi bridge, near the epicenter and he left Sgt. Atkinson there. Sgt. Atkinson died around noon on Aug. 7, 1995 [this date is obviously a typographical error that was intended to read 1945]. Soon after he died. A photographer, Mr. Toshiaki Sasaki dicovered the body of Sgt. Atkinson and he told that he stood there and watched the body for about an hour. According to the witness of Mr. Sasaki, there was no sign of abuse on Sgt. Atkinson, the body was intact.

### Julius Molnar

He was a tail gunner on the *Taloa*, a B-24 on the same flight with the *Lonesome Lady* and also shot down. The Adjutant General's office, in a letter to his mother dated May 15, 1946, wrote her "to inform you of the death of your son . . . who was previously reported missing in action 28 July 1945." The initial report stated that his bomber was shot down over Kyushu. Later, on February 10, 1949, she was informed that "Department of Army records are, therefore, being corrected to show that Staff Sergeant Molnar was killed in action on 6 August 1945 at Hiroshima, Honshu, Japan . . ."

A mass funeral for eight men was held November 3, 1949, at Jefferson Barracks National Cemetery in St. Louis, Missouri. The services consisted of burying one symbolic casket. Only the dates of death and names were listed on the tombstone. Five of these eight were from the *Lonesome Lady*: Atkinson, Ellison, Long, Looper, and Ryan. Their death date, along with that of Baumgartner from the *Taloa* and Porter, the pilot of the Hellcat from the USS *Ticonderoga*, was listed as August 6, 1945. The other name listed was that of Molnar, whose death date was listed as July 28, 1945. The July 28 date is of course in variance with the statement above which indicates that the death date was "corrected" to August 6, 1945. Whether Molnar survived until August 6 is in question.

## Relevant Stories

There are several sidebar stories that relate to the fateful mission of the *Lonesome Lady*. I call the first one *Taloa*, the second *Haruna*, the third *A Small Piece of the "Lady" Who Flew Back Home as a Peace Dove*, and the last is *The Indefatigable Mr. Mori*.

## The *Taloa*

As mentioned above, flying in the same squadron on the *Haruna* mission, the *Taloa* was also a casualty. The lead plane was flown by Emil Turek; we were on his left wing, and then Joe Dubinsky and crew followed below in the *Taloa*. Turek's plane was hit by an anti-aircraft shell just before bomb release, which caused a fuel leak. Just after bombs away, the *Taloa* was hit by several of the many anti-aircraft shells thrown up at us. We were hit only seconds after the *Taloa*. Turek's plane made it back to an intermediate base (Ie Shima). Dubinsky's plane had taken three or four direct hits; it swung off to the left under our squadron and then went into a steep dive as seen and reported by the bombardier Nacci on Turek's plane. Five of the eleven aboard were seen to bail out; the remaining six were reported to have gone down with the plane, which crashed into a hillside close to Hiroshima. Dubinsky, the last to get out, was too late. According to the official U.S. military report, he hit the ground before his chute opened (more about Dubinsky's fate below). Walter Piskor, engineer, landed on the roof of a Mitsubishi plant where he was taken by civilians, thrown from the building, and killed. Rudolph C. Flanagin, copilot, landed in the Ota River, was captured by fishermen, and beaten to death. Charles Baumgartner and Julius Molnar, both gunners, survived their jump, came down close together, and were taken by a hostile civilian crowd. The military police arrived on the scene just in time to save them but only with much effort. They were taken into Hiroshima to the Chugoku Military Police Headquarters. The records are not clear, but it appears likely that these two did not survive their internment long enough to be alive August 6, when the atomic bomb was dropped. Neither are listed on the Hiroshima POW Memorial Project tablet at the Andersonville Prisoner of War Museum, which includes names of those "who lost their lives while prisoners of war at Hiroshima, Japan, the day of the bomb, August 6, 1945."

### The *Haruna*

The *Haruna,* as mentioned above, was a ghost battleship since it had been reported to have been sunk by Col. Colin Kelly of the Air Force in a fatal dive bombing in the badly crippled B-17 that he was piloting. Maj. Edwin Halter, Operations Officer, 494th Bombardment Group, wrote in a letter to me dated March 12, 1985, that he briefed the entire B-24 mission to Kure Harbor, which included groups other than the 494th. He wrote that "I did not like the mission due to the fact that GP (general personnel) bombs, which is all we had, were inadequate to sink a battleship the size of the *Haruna* . . . When this fact was known it was not very well received and I got the distinct impression that the Army wanted to 'beat' the Navy. As a matter of fact, when the mission was scrubbed a day or so earlier due to inclement weather, Col. [Lawrence] Kelley [Commanding Officer of the 494th ] was highly annoyed because he wanted to 'scoop' the Navy. The attitude going around, as I remember it, was that 'Col. Lawrence Kelley will sink the battleship that Colin Kelley missed'."

According to a surviving *Haruna* crew member, Mr. Mitsumine, the *Haruna* had been harbor bound since February because it had transferred all of its fuel to other war ships in light of the dire fuel shortage of the Japanese. The sunken *Haruna* rested on the bottom of Kure Harbor with the superstructure protruding for several years after the war until it was salvaged—to be put out of sight, according to the surviving crew member.

### A Small Piece of the "Lady" Who Flew Back Home as a Peace Dove

In 1985 I received a letter dated July 12 from Mr. Keiichi Muranaka, principal of Tenno Junior High School in Iwakuni City, about forty kilometers from Hiroshima. After courteous greetings, he explained that he had been drafted into the Japanese Navy and was waiting on shore to be stationed on one of "only two ships hold up in Kure Harbour [there were more ships in this general area, but Mr. Muranaka was apparently referring to a more specific area] . . . when we took part in the attack . . . on July 28, 1945." He stated that he saw our damaged, smoking plane go over and knew that the crew bailed out and that the plane crashed. "A few days later on July 6, 1945, the A-Bomb was dropped on Hiroshima. I can still remember the sight of the mushroom cloud spreading over the city. When I returned home on August 26, 1945, I encountered the remains of a wrecked B-24. I realized that the wreckage was part of the same B-24 which I had seen [going down on July 28]. I picked up a piece of that wreckage to keep as a remainder [reminder] of the war." In December of 1984 he learned from a newspaper article "that the name of the plane was '*Lonesome Lady*' and the chief pilot was you Dr. Cartwright. Moreover you were the only survivor and had a narrow escape from death [of course, Bill Abel also survived]."

Mr. Muranaka goes on to write that "Forty years have passed since the crash of your plane . . . The U.S. and Japan has overcome the difficulties caused by the war. Friendly relations between our countries has been improving. This pleases me greatly. I could not imagine the peace we enjoy today when I was in the Navy. I always relate my sad experiences regarding WW II and A-Bomb and the crash of the '*Lonesome Lady*'. I also show them my memento of the crash. Now I would like to give you this article which I have kept all these years as a reminder of the sad experiences we shared during that terrible time in history. By remembering we shall be able to maintain this peace we enjoy now. This is our responsibility." The article referred to in the quotation is the part of the *Lonesome Lady* that he picked up at the crash site; it is a piece of aluminum, irregularly shaped, about nine inches long and ranging from about three to five inches wide, and obviously torn loose in the crash.

I was emotionally overwhelmed. Though meager, this twisted piece of metal was something solid, palpable, related to memories of my crew that had been lacking—they had vanished, with only my speculation, for so long. Also, I was touched by the symbolic part of the *Lady* flying back home as a peace dove. I responded to Mr. Muranaka, thanking him for the "memento," which was very touching to me and greatly treasured—he must have parted with his treasure reluctantly. I also briefly told him about my family and career. He wrote back, "I was very impressed by the thoughtful words in your letter. Forty years ago I retrieved the piece of B-24 though my behavior was unlawful . . . Although the wreckage is only a small part of the B-24, which had come here over the Pacific Ocean and had gotten through the fire of our anti-aircraft guns," I return it with the "sincere hope that this piece of wreckage will deepen our mutual friendship and contribute to our lasting peace." He went on to invite me to return to visit the crash site with him as my guide.

In 1997 Mr. Muranaka requested permission to have a memoir that I had written earlier, entitled *A Date With The Lonesome Lady*, translated into Japanese to be placed in a small museum in the village of Ikachi, which is close to the crash site. Also he initiated an effort to raise funds to place a monument at the site in memory of all military who gave their lives in the war' and to specifically honor the memory of the airmen of the *Lonesome Lady* who gave their lives in Japan.

### The Indefatigable Mr. Mori

Mr. Mori was an eight-year-old school boy in Hiroshima on August 6, 1945. He survived because he was sick that day and had been sent to the outskirts of the city instead of to the center to work as usual. As a "hibakusha" (a Japanese term translated as "explosion affected person") he has health problems associated with radiation effects. As an historian he has become very interested in the historical record of the crew of the *Lonesome Lady* and other U.S. airmen interned in Hiroshima. He has traveled to the site of the crash to take pictures and interview people who were alive at that time.

Through these acquaintances he has arranged for them to send me many pieces that their families had gathered from the wreckage of the *Lonesome Lady*. Also, he has searched for and found many obscure records as well as conducted interviews with various officials with knowledge about incidents concerning my crew and other POWs interned in Hiroshima. He has corresponded with Jim Ryan's brother Francis and contributed relevant articles to Japanese newspapers, magazines, and TV stations.

The Chugoku Military Police Headquarters building where U.S. POWs were held in Hiroshima was completely destroyed by the atomic bomb and was later replaced by a modern office building. Mr. Mori got permission from the current owner to place a plaque on this building. The plaque is inscribed with a brief memorial statement that he requested that I write, along with the names of the U.S. airmen incarcerated there when the A-bomb was dropped. He had committed himself to work extra hours after his retirement in order to earn money to finance this project and its dedication (over a million yen). The inscription on the plaque reads:

> The atomic bomb dropped on Hiroshima August 6, 1945, devastated the city and its people with a force beyond any known before. U.S. Army Air Corps and U.S. Navy Airmen interned as POWs at Chugoku Military Police Headquarters which was located at this site, near the epicenter, were among the victims of this holocaust. This plaque is placed in memory of these brave and honorable men. May this humble memorial be a perpetual reminder of the savagery of war.

Among the documents that Mr. Mori has found are microfilms of the official records that the Japanese government was ordered by the U.S. Occupation Force to produce for each POW interned in Japan. These were required to be translated into English. One about me was submitted by the Japanese Home Defense Corps through the Japan Demobilization Bureau concerning captured airmen in the Hiroshima area. It is inaccurate in detail but is of interest at least to me. It was dated December 27, 1946, and reads:

Name: Thomas Charles Cartwright (American), Rank: 2nd Lt.
Date of Capture: July 28, 1945
Place of Capture: Ikachi Village. Kuga District, Yamaguchi Prefecture
Capturers: Members of the Ikachi Civilian Anti-Air Corps (particulars unknown)

Escorts: M.P. Corporal Kotaro Tsujii, Leading Private Masaru Tsubota, 1st Private Yutaka Matsumura, 1st Private Haruhiko Kajita, M.P. Sergeant Mataichi Katashima, M.P. Sergeant Ryoji Yanagihara.

Circumstances of Capture and Subsequent Process: He was the commander of the above mentioned plane [identified earlier by number, etc.] and made a parachute descent, but was caught by some members of the Iroku Village Civilian Anti-Air-Raid Corps at 3:30 P.M. on July 28. He was protected by the Yanai Police Station. Afterward Yanai Military Police Sub-Section received him and sent him to Chugoku Military Police General Headquarters [Hiroshima] on 29th. He was again sent to Imperial General Headquarters, Tokyo, leaving Hiroshima on July 30. He was delivered to the Eastern 186th Unit. He ought to have returned to his country already.

## Conclusions

There has been much written about the decision of whether to drop an atomic bomb on Japan and where to drop it. Without debating the larger issues here, it should be noted that, according to historian Barton Bernstein, "Hiroshima was chosen as the first target city for the A-bomb because it did not seem to have any POW camp." Bernstein also notes that Gen. Carl Spatz, commanding general of the Army Air Force in the Pacific, in response to inquiry, cabled Washington: "If you consider your information reliable Hiroshima should be given first priority . . . Information available here indicates that there are prisoner of war camps in practically every major Japanese city." Spatz and Washington knew, according to Bernstein, that an official list of "Locations and Strengths of Prisoner of War Camps . . . in Japan" listed a camp in Hiroshima based on a 1944 British report. There appears to be no doubt that effort was made to avoid, or at least minimize, harming our own by "friendly fire."

Several conclusions are clearly supported by the facts and circumstances stated above. One is that six of the *Lonesome Lady* crew were indeed in Hiroshima and killed that August 6, or within a few days, either by the direct explosion/heat effects of the atomic bomb or by its radiation effects or by the Japanese while dying from these bomb effects. Second, the U.S. military officials did report to next of kin that they were killed in Hiroshima on or shortly after August 6, 1945. The military did not acknowledge that the cause of death was direct or indirect effects of the atomic bomb. Whether this failure to specify cause of death was simply the nature of military to state only specifically known facts or was intentional to downplay the fact that we dropped an atomic bomb on some of our own personnel is a matter of conjecture. Certainly the delayed notifications to families—and the fact that the full story of known facts was not made public until the media, especially a dedicated documentary filmmaker named Gary DeWalt, dug out the truth after the Freedom of Information Act was passed—caused a great deal of anxiety among families and friends. As well, it was a disservice to all Americans. In any event it does not reflect well on either the competence or compassion of our military leaders whom these men, caught in Hiroshima, had trusted and served with complete dedication. (A similar procedure of delayed and scant information that the War Department provided families of POWs killed in Japan is reported in the book *Shobun, A Forgotten War Crime in the Pacific* by Michael Goodwin.)

### Reflections

I have reflected for a half century on the events that I have attempted to faithfully record here with objectivity. Going through the various events in this writing, an array of emotions and memories swept over me at various times. One was the memory of the thrill, at eighteen years and full of vigor and curiosity, of leaving a small southern town, and of an uninspired start at college to experience places in Florida, Texas, California, Virginia, Hawaii, etc.; to meet people from New York, Pennsylvania, Iowa, Michigan, Wisconsin, etc.; to learn to fly, earn my wings and commission, and to become a pilot of a four-engine plane and commander of a ten-man crew, all enhanced by the opportunity of flying.

Another memory was that of the satisfying fraternity of our crew. We had professional pride and always were graded "excellent" and one time "superior" after coolly responding to having an engine shot out by an errant gunner during a towed target practice. We never got drunk or caroused but enjoyed every assignment for whatever it had to offer.

From the time that the anti-aircraft shell damaged our plane until we were in custody of the military, through bailout, turning myself in, civilian harassment, and interrogation, I think that I kept control of my feelings and actions. Perhaps a small thing but still very vivid in my memory is that when the farmer had taken me to a local police station and I had turned in my pistol, my mouth was so very dry, as was Looper's, that we ventured to ask for water from our inhospitable hosts. Yet, I do not remember having the feeling of being scared. When I was blindfolded, escorted to a drill field, pushed to my knees with head down, I did not have feelings of panic. I knew from that time on that I could face death with equanimity. After that experience, when the harassment had stopped and I sat in my solitary cell, I decided that what I wanted to seek in life was, first, to marry my sweetheart when I got home and, second, to become a peaceful farmer. I accomplished the first and came close to the second.

Whenever I thought of the meeting with Bill Abel back on Okinawa, shaking hands and hugging spontaneously over and over, thinking that the rest of our crew, our buddies, were on their way—just hadn't gotten there yet—I would choke up and my eyes would get misty, just as they are as I write this.

On the fiftieth anniversary of the dropping of the atomic bomb on Hiroshima, several TV program producers and newspaper writers contacted me in order to include my experience in their stories. One question asked by all of these people was whether I thought the United States should have dropped the atomic bombs on Japan. When I asked them for the rationale for asking me, a geneticist, this question, their answer was always related only to the fact that I was closely involved. I refused to express my opinion, which seemed to perplex them. They assumed that I did not hold an opinion. But that is not correct. I am one of few Americans who had family or close friends killed by the atomic bomb—that fact perhaps gives me a different perspective to view the decision to employ the bomb on a populated area. Also, dropping the bomb, rather than invading the Japanese mainland, undoubtedly saved my life. There is sufficient documentation to clearly establish the fact that Japanese commanders of POW camps and holding prisons had "shobun" orders on their desks to immediately execute, preferably by beheading, all allied prisoners if an invasion of the main Japanese Islands was initiated. The practice of beheading POWs by the military was practiced, sometimes almost as a spectator sport, and this order is entirely believable.

Given the time and circumstances of July/August 1945, I agree with most of the historians who experienced those times directly. For many reasons (which are all well documented) there was no real option available to President Truman and his advisors other than demonstrating that we had atomic bombs and that these bombs had devastating power. The only real points to debate, in my opinion, are whether the two atomic bombs, "Little Boy" and "Fat Man," should have been employed as they were. In retrospect, it is clear to me that the U.S. should not have employed the first atomic bomb in the densely populated Hiroshima area. It is also now evident to me that the second bomb should not have been dropped so soon, and again on the populated area of Nagasaki, before the Japanese Cabinet had time, given their structure and customs which were known to our decision makers, to reach a decision (a clear, quick, unanimous consensus of the Japanese War Cabinet was probably not possible) to accept surrender terms which may not have been clearly stated or clearly understood by the Japanese.

As indicated above, I have made acquaintances, via correspondence with two Japanese men, Mr. Keiichi Muranaka, who witnessed the mushroom cloud and the aftermath of the atomic bomb, and Mr. Shigeaki Mori, a "hibakusha" (explosion affected person). Particularly since making these acquaintances, I have come to realize that I am one of a fairly small group of Americans who share the devastating experiences of many Japanese of having had dearly cherished, close friends killed by the atomic bomb. How could I possibly not have mixed emotions?

The carnage in the Pacific area of WW II, with which I was directly and indirectly familiar, includes the decisions made by our generals and admirals to continue attacking a disabled Japanese fleet apparently in order to revenge earlier defeats at the inevitable cost of lives. Disturbing is the cruelty and inhumane treatment inflicted by the Japanese military on enemy civilians and POWs; the fanaticism of "kamikaze" pilots and the "bushido" and "shobun" mentality encouraged by the Japanese military and its consequences; and the devastating and lasting carnage of bombing civilian areas with fire bombs and atomic bombs. When I reflected on these atrocities, I wondered if civilization had progressed from ancient times.

Almost equally disturbing is the almost instant about-face of the Japanese people, except for some of the older, hardened military fanatics, to revert instantly to a friendly demeanor when the emperor announced that they were surrendering—disturbing in that it seems that the human spirit can be turned on and off. Can they (we) be made to revert to animalistic behavior without a conscience?

Surely, only war can revert a people to such inflamed hatred of the enemy "tribe." Surely, only by avoiding war can we expect ourselves and others to progress up the evolving civilization scale to the moral point that we like to think our great religions represent. War can be avoided only if we are willing to understand and accept others and if we are willing to help them or accept help from them; that is, we must be willing to interact with one another, to get to know each other, and to share among countries as members of an extended family share in both good times and bad.

Lt. Tom Cartwright illegally (under age) in a Los Angeles bar in 1944.

The B-24 crew of Tom Cartwright before departing for the Pacific.

*Mr. Seiichi Tamai in 1965. He was the person the author first encountered in Japan after parachuting from the* Lonesome Lady *and is credited with "capturing" him.*
—Courtesy Mr. Shigeaki Mori

*Bill Abel and the author in 1998 at Bill's home in Colorado. These are the two survivors of the* Lonesome Lady *who were shot down, captured, and imprisoned.*

*POWs at Omori Prison Camp enthusiastically welcoming Marines on landing barges coming to clandestinely liberate them on August 28, 1945, before the surrender document was signed. The author's head is seen at the right edge of this picture poking through the mob. The POWs shown are the ones who were strong enough to physically celebrate; the ones who were skeletons with skin hanging on them could barely leave their pallets.*

—Courtesy National Archives

*The author shortly after repatriation in September 1945, visiting his outfit during a short stay at his Okinawa base on his return to the U.S. He is dressed in clothes provided by the navy.*

—Courtesy a friend, Lt. Truman Thursten, Navigator

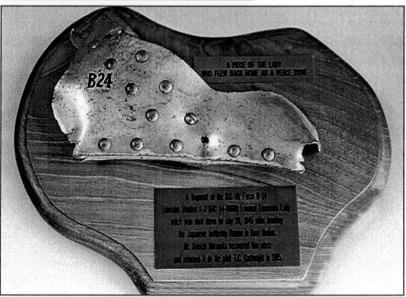

*A fragment from the crashed* Lonesome Lady *recovered by Mr. Keiichi Muranaka from the crash site in 1945 and returned in 1985 to the author, who mounted it as a keepsake.*

*Mr. Shigeaki Mori, Shinto priests in the background, at the dedication ceremony for the Memorial Plaque that he had erected in 1998 honoring American POWs killed in Hiroshima by the atomic bomb.*

—Courtesy Mr. Mori

*Mr. Mitsumine Hisahiro, president of the Battleship Haruna Veterans, and Maj. Timothy Keefe, U.S. Marine from the Iwakuni U.S. Naval Base, unveiling the Memorial Plaque that Mr. Mori had placed at the former site of the Chugoku Military Police Headquarters Building.*

—Courtesy Mr. Mori

*Memorial Plaque erected at the former site of the Chugoku Military Police Headquarters in Hiroshima where American POWs were held when the atomic bomb was dropped. The names of the known victims, including six from the* Lonesome Lady, *are inscribed on the plaque in English. It was conceived, financed, and dedicated by Mr. Shigeaki Mori of Hiroshima.*

—Courtesy Mr. Mori

*The Memorial Plaque dedicated to American airmen killed in Hiroshima.*

—Courtesy Mr. Mori

*Pat Cartwright, Carolyn Cartwright, the author, and Matt Crawford at the Cenotaph of the Memorial Peace Park in Hiroshima. They have just placed flowers at this centerpiece of the Park during their return visit in 1999.*

*The Atomic Memorial Mound in the Peace Memorial Park in Hiroshima, where remains, mostly ashes, of atomic bomb victims were buried en masse. The remains of some of the author's* Lonesome Lady *crew may have been buried here.*

*The Japanese battleship* Haruna *resting on the bottom of Kure Harbor after the air raids on July 28, 1945, in which the* Lonesome Lady *took part. Anti-aircraft fire from this ship probably shot down the* Lonesome Lady.

*A monument erected by the survivors of the Japanese battleship* Haruna *dedicated to those who perished when intensively bombed by the* Lonesome Lady *and others in late July 1945. In the foreground are Dr. Pat Cartwright, Mr. Shigeaki Mori, the author, his wife Carolyn, Mr. Mitsumine Hisahiro, Mr. Matt Crawford, and Mr. Kondo Takeyoshi. Mr. Mitsumine and Mr. Kondo were crew members of the* Haruna, *who shot at us on July 28, 1945.*

*Mr. Mitsumine demonstrating to the author, through an interpreter, how the U.S. Air Force and U.S. Navy planes came in and bombed his ship, the port-bound battleship* Haruna.

*Mr. Muneo Okabe, a Buddhist priest, explaining his witnessing as an eight-year-old boy the crashing of the* Taloa *in a suburb of Hiroshima. This B-24 was in the same flight as the* Lonesome Lady *and was piloted by Lt. Joe Dubinsky. An interpreter, the author and his wife, and Mr. Shigeaka Mori looking on.*

*The author, his wife Carolyn and son Pat enjoying a traditional Japanese dinner as guests of their Japanese hosts in 1999.*

*Carolyn Cartwright placing flowers at the Shinto altar in the home of Mrs. Mika Marumo, who witnessed the parachuting of one of the* Lonesome Lady *crew and the subsequent shooting of her father by this soldier. The records of the identity of this crew member were burned when Hiroshima was bombed; he was to be tried for murder.*

*A rice farmer, in boots, who as a boy witnessed four of the* Lonesome Lady *crew parachute, explains where he saw them come down. Shown are the TV crew and a newspaper reporter behind the farmer, who is facing Mr. Muranaka and the author, with Matt Crawford taking a picture.*

*A "photo op" of the welcoming party at Ikachi. The tip of the monument is seen at the right of the sign.*

*Mr. Keiichi Muranaka at the welcoming reception held at Ikachi. He sent the piece of the* Lonesome Lady *that initiated the author's interest in returning to Japan.*

*The monument placed at the village of Ikachi in 1998 close to the rice paddy where* Lonesome Lady *crashed. One side is dedicated to all who perished in the war. The other side is dedicated to the* Lonesome Lady *crew and lists their names, both those who perished in Japan and those who lived to be repatriated.*

*The author reading his "Letter to the People of Ikachi," wife Carolyn on left, son Pat holding plaque, and Matt Crawford. The sign reads "Dr. T. C. Cartwright Welcome To Ikachi."*

*Carolyn Cartwright holding flowers presented to her by Mrs. Teruko Fujinaka at the welcoming ceremony for the Cartwrights' visit to Ikachi.*

*Mrs. Teruko Fujinaka and a Shinto priest at the dedication ceremony for the monument (in background) erected at Ikachi in 1998. Mrs Fujinaka was very instrumental in having the monument funded and erected and is the author of* The Fallen B-24 [the Lonesome Lady].

—Courtesy Mr. Keiichi Muranaka.

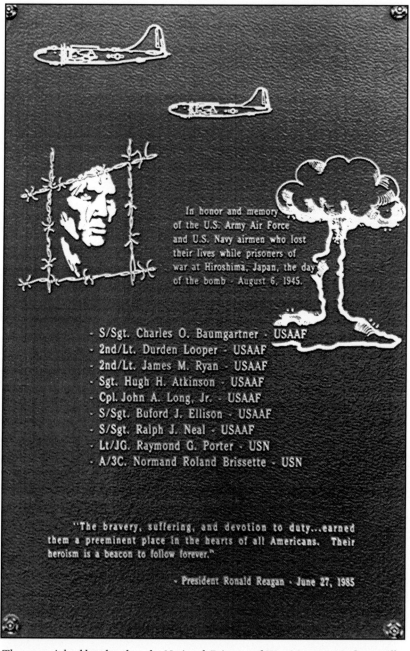

*The memorial tablet placed at the National Prisoner of War Museum, Andersonville, Georgia, honoring American POWs killed in Hiroshima by the atomic bomb.*

—Courtesy the Andersonville National Historic Site

# Chapter Three

# A RETURN TO HIROSHIMA

## Earlier Visits

My first trip to Japan as a POW was, to say the least, unpleasant. I entered and left Hiroshima with hands tied and blindfolded and saw little more than the inside of a prison cell and an interrogation room. I saw almost nothing while being transferred to the Imperial Military Headquarters, Tokyo, and only a prison cell and interrogation room while there. I saw nothing while being transferred to the Omori POW camp and very little after being freed of blindfolds and a prison cell. Physical and mental harassment bordered on abuse but, except for one occasion, was not severe. Rations were very meager; I lost a pound per day, my joints had begun to ache, and my gums became too tender to chew hard. I was comparatively fortunate as a Japanese POW and especially fortunate that my stay in Japan was not fatal, as I escaped a number of situations that were potentially hazardous, some very close calls, especially based on the experiences of other POWs.

My next trip to Japan was in August 1983, when I was invited to give a paper at a beef genetics conference in Kyoto. I arrived a few days early in order to catch the train to Hiroshima to visit the place where I was imprisoned and, more importantly, to set foot on the ground where six of my crew were killed by the atomic bomb. I do not know what I expected to do except walk around the places where these events likely took place. Also, I wanted to visit the Hiroshima Peace Memorial Museum and thought of introducing myself to the museum director. I arrived late at night and got a room at the closest hotel to the train station.

The next morning I slept late after a trans-Pacific flight followed by a train ride from Tokyo. About midmorning I braced myself and walked around, observing the remains of a building where I thought we had been interned. I stood for a while looking at the A-Bomb Dome building, the rather dramatic preserved remains of the steel skeleton of a domed building. Then I went to the Peace Memorial Park and lingered at the Cenotaph, the focal point of the park, where the names of deceased victims of the atomic bomb are kept in a vault and added to each year on August 6. From there I went to the large park museum.

In the museum, after the first few glimpses of the gruesome depiction of the city's destruction and life-size models and pictures of people horribly burned and otherwise maimed, with my mind full of memories of my comrades who died there, and perhaps feelings of "survivor's guilt," these displays were repulsive to me. Also, the presentations seemed to be unfairly accusatory of the U.S. without any background information or rationale for the atomic bomb being employed.

I turned on my heel to leave this behind. I had never been conscious of any survivor guilt feelings, but my feelings took over, perhaps being reinforced by jet lag, and I could not bear to remain there. I headed for the train station.

In my somber mood, an incongruous incident happened. As I was striding across the park, I noted that a large number of schoolchildren were visiting the park, all clustered in groups. Then a school girl from one of the groups, about twelve years old, I guess, ran over to me with a bunch of girl classmates following. In very understandable but classroom English, she asked with a big smile, "May I ask you some questions?" I could not hurt a pleasant young girl's feelings. She asked the usual questions written on her sheet, such as "Where are you from?" After each answer she gushed out "thank you" and each of her friends recorded answers after a short discussion in Japanese. Then she said, "One last question, thank you—have you ever been in Hiroshima before and if so when?" I answered, "Yes, in early August 1945." I left wondering whether her teacher would reprimand her and her classmates for writing down a date that was obviously incorrect. My mind was not clear enough then to be specific about dates, but the last day in 1945 that I was in Hiroshima was probably July 30.

### Peace Offerings

The repulsive feeling lingering from my visit to Hiroshima taunted my mind for years after August 1983. I began to have better feelings when Mr. Keiichi Muranaka wrote to me wishing for continued peace and sent me the fragment of the *Lonesome Lady*, as described in the previous chapter. We corresponded a number of times and I began to feel that I had a friend in Japan who was familiar with, and involved in, the history of my crew in Japan. Then in 1995 Mr. Shigeaki Mori wrote and started a lasting correspondence (more details of the "indefatigable" Mr. Mori were covered earlier). My feelings had mellowed much by this time. And with details of the missing history of me and my crew in Japan discovered and relayed to me by Mr. Mori, I felt that I now had two real friends in Japan.

From his own inspiration and through his own efforts and expense, Mr. Mori had a plaque made and erected in 1998 at the site where my crew was interned when the atomic bomb was dropped. It was dedicated to the ten U.S. Air Force and Navy Airmen known at that time to have been killed there. Mr. Muranaka had inspired the erection of a monument in 1998 in the village of Ikachi which honored the deceased of my crew.

Gradually, the thought of returning to Japan became appealing to me in order to meet these gracious people and to visit the sites of the memorial plaque in Hiroshima and the memorial monument in Ikachi village.

I now had friends who wanted me to come to Japan and wanted to be my guide and show me things relevant to me and my crew. I think that they also wanted to meet me.

After being showered by parts recovered from the *Lonesome*

*Lady* sent to me, through Mr. Mori, by the local citizens of Ikachi, and getting a booklet that a lady my age, Mrs. Teruko Fujinaka, had written about *The Fallen B-24*, plans for a return trip began to foment. The booklet was Mrs. Fujinaka's account of the crashing of the *Lonesome Lady* and of her sighting of me and Copilot Looper parachuting. She had conducted extensive interviews of others who were witnesses to the fall and capture of other crew members. Also, she had requested a copy of my "memoirs" (written before this revision); it was translated into Japanese and she read its translation. She used this translation to help convince her friends in this close-knit village to erect the monument in Ikachi dedicated on one side to "the many people killed or severely damaged in the war" and on the other side specifically to my crew who died in Japan and to the two survivors (Bill Abel and me). By the time all of these items were received and digested, my desire to return cascaded to a compelling urge.

## A Pilgrimage

Definite plans were made through our Japanese friends who had invited us and wanted to host us, taking care of all arrangements, for Carolyn, my wife, and me to visit Hiroshima and Ikachi. Our younger son, Dr. Pat Cartwright, asked to join us as soon as he learned of our plans. Matt Crawford, president of the 494th Bomb Group (H) Association, the veterans organization of my group, also asked to join us. After dozens of e-mails to Mr. Mori, who coordinated with Mr. Muranaka, a very interesting and appropriate itinerary was set. Dr. Paul Satoh, a native of Hiroshima and school classmate and friend of Mr. Mori, who has been a successful research pharmacist in the U.S. most of his adult life, translated e-mail and fax messages between Mr. Mori and me. Without his efficient and talented efforts, as well as counsel, the trip would not have gone as smoothly. We all blanched several times when we would get information about the dollar falling against the yen and about prices in Japan, but no one thought of backing out.

The purpose of my visit was to meet and thank the people who had erected a plaque and monument acknowledging my crew and other U.S. airmen, and who had dug out much history about my crew and corresponded with me. Also, at the appropriate places and times, we wanted to pay homage to my comrades who died there, and especially to my crew, all of whom were my close friends. There were other things of interest, such as meeting the U.S. Marine, Major Keefe, who participated in the dedication of the memorial plaque Mr. Mori had conceived and erected. Of course we were interested in seeing some of the Japanese culture, their religious shrines, the rebuilt city of Hiroshima, etc. We expected to be involved only with those with whom we had become acquainted through correspondence and a few others they might introduce.

Our party of four met at the Los Angeles airport and flew nonstop to Kansai Airport at Osaka, the closest international airport to Hiroshima. We were met there by a television crew from NHK (the national TV network in Japan) Hiroshima. They were there for the purpose of escorting us to our hotel for the night to rest from the long flight and diurnal reversal of day and night times. The next morning they escorted us through a rather complex set of railway exchanges and on to a "bullet train" to Hiroshima. This crew followed us almost every place that we went and were very polite and considerate. We became friends with them as the trip progressed, and they were very helpful at times, but also not hesitant to ask us to "pose" or repeat certain things. As the first part of the TV documentary they were producing of our trip, they posed me by a window on the bullet train and asked me questions as the country flashed by at 120 to 150 MPH on our way to Hiroshima. Matt had his camcorder going, and Pat took photos to start their own documentation of our trip.

By this time we were aware that our visit would not go unnoticed by others than our hosts, but we were not prepared for arrival at the Hiroshima train station. Our train and car number had been faxed ahead. As we stepped off, other TV crews, perhaps a half dozen or more newspaper reporters with their cameramen, as well as Mr. and Mrs. Mori, Mr. Muranaka, translators, and others were there in what at first appeared to us to be a melee. I have little recollection of what went on there, except a lot of handshaking. We were then escorted to our hotel—a very nice new hotel with excellent service.

A quite astute young lady, Mrs. Atsuko Shigesawa, then editor for the Hiroshima Peace Institute, who was present for all of our meetings and often interpreted for us, noted that we were a bit dismayed at all of the attention. She explained to me that Mr. Mori, a friend whom she recognized as a very knowledgeable historian, was a very humble and conscientious person. He had dedicated so much of his time and energy into research to find and record the history of U.S. airmen in Hiroshima that it was impossible for him to not be inspired by our presence. He pulled strings and put a great deal of effort into making arrangements for us that would make our visit most meaningful. Also, Mr. Muranaka, in coordination with Mr. Mori, arranged a very meaningful visit for us to the area where we parachuted and were captured before being sent to Hiroshima.

At the hotel we had tea after checking in, and at that time we were introduced to Mr. Tatsoru Tsukamae, seventy-eight years old, who had been a policeman stationed near Aioi Bridge in August 1945. He told the story about walking across Aioi Bridge after the atomic bomb had been dropped and seeing the very sick Sergeant Atkinson, radio operator of the *Lonesome Lady*, and sharing his limited water with him. Since Sergeant Atkinson died on this bridge either from being beaten or from radiation effects, this gesture by a man that Mr. Mori had somehow found was Mr. Mori's way, I believe, of setting the stage for us to have open minds.

### POW Memorial

The first place on our schedule was to visit the memorial plaque that Mr. Mori had placed at the site of Chugoku Military Headquarters Building. We had expected to pay homage, in our own way, to our fallen comrades—six from my crew, two from the 494th *Taloa*, and two navy airmen. When Hiroshima was rebuilt, this turned out to be an office building on a small street. All of the media people who were at the train station also turned up there and crowded around this shrine. There was nothing to do except for the four of us to line up, place flowers at the plaque, and bow reverently while the TV and camera crews scrambled to get shots and ask us questions. We came back to this memorial site later at the request of the NHK TV director, whom we had come to respect, so he could get clear shots.

I had written a letter to Mr. Mori that I had intended to hand to him in private. I summarized the things he had done that I deeply appreciated, especially having the plaque placed at this most meaningful place, and thanked him for his dedication. He had handed me a letter of appreciation for making the trip when I arrived at the train station, so I decided to read my letter to him at this meeting so that the media present could give him due credit.

Dear Mr. Mori,

It is my great pleasure to be able to meet you in person and thank you for the many things you have done to honor our comrades and to clarify the history of their fate. Your dedication to history, both in revealing events and correcting the record of events is most noteworthy. The time, energy and funds that you have put into this history is beyond our imagination, but we do appreciate and acknowledge your efforts knowing that they were extraordinary.

You have enlightened me about many events related to the *Lonesome Lady* being shot down and the fate of my crew and the other American Airmen held in Hiroshima.

For some time after the war I still did not know the fate of my crew except for the two of us who survived and some terse telegrams from the U.S. War Department to the families of the others. The loss of close comrades, who had all become like family members, confirmed only by time and brief reports, some of which I knew to be erroneous, was a very uncomfortable, unsettling memory. The film *Genbaku Shi* reported positive information about the deaths of those held in Hiroshima. Only now, over 50 years later, do I believe that most of the details are now known and recorded thanks to your untiring efforts. Although this knowledge does not change the past, it does correct the recorded history and, for me personally, in my retirement, which is a time of memories and reflection, I rest easier knowing that the truth is known.

Also of great comfort to me and the families of our comrades is the recognition given to their memory by the plaque you have created and placed at the most appropriate place. Not only is this plaque recognition of the heroic deaths of U.S. Airmen, it serves to remind our sons and their sons of the horrors of war and the benefits of peace.

For these many things, I express heartfelt appreciation for myself but also for the families of the deceased. The two of us have developed, I believe, a friendship through correspondence—now we can confirm it face to face with a hardy handshake.

With respect and gratitude, Tom Cartwright

On another day we asked the TV crew and reporters not to follow us so that we could return to the memorial plaque in order to simply observe, alone with our own feelings, the place where our comrades were killed by the atomic bomb. We stood silently for a long while, paying homage, in our own way, to our comrades.

### Hiroshima Haunts

The next day we left the hotel for a long stroll through historic sites of importance to us. First was the Chugoku Military Police Headquarters, where six of my crew and I were held and interrogated. Along the way we stopped at a marker signifying the "hypocenter" (the point directly under the point of detonation, which was 1,890 feet above ground level) of the atomic explosion. Then on to the famous (infamous) Aioi Bridge, a very unique structure that in 1945 was shaped like the letter T where a smaller bridge joined a larger bridge near its center (it has now been rebuilt in the same general shape). This unique bridge was the sighting point for the bombardier, Maj. Thomas Ferebee, of the *Enola Gay,* who said that "It's the most perfect AP I've seen in this whole damn war." The epicenter of the bomb missed centering over Aioi Bridge by 800 feet.

One of my crew was reportedly taken to the badly damaged Aioi Bridge after the bombing, tied to lamp post, and killed as described above. Even though this event seems to be well documented, there has been an alternative explanation offered. His body was buried about a dozen feet from the bridge on the banks of the river. We placed flowers at his unmarked gravesite. The NHK TV crew was still with us but it was not hectic, and although we posed some, we could reflect meaningfully on the memory of our unfortunate comrade that I believe was Sgt. Hugh Atkinson.

## Hiroshima Museum

From there we walked to the Peace Memorial Park and Museum. First we observed a common burial ground, a large mound of earth, for the ashes of thousands killed by the atomic bomb—ashes of some of our comrades were probably placed there. Next was the Cenotaph, which is the centerpiece of the park. It is a ceramic monument shaped like an open slice out of a narrow, tall Quonset. It covers a tomb that holds a sealed vault, which holds a register of names of all who are known as "gen-shibaku-dansho," those who were killed or mortally injured by the atomic bomb. It is opened on the anniversary of the dropping of the bomb each year to add new names. Through the efforts of Mr. Mori, families of several of the *Lonesome Lady* crew have had the names of their loved ones entered there.

At the Hiroshima Peace Memorial Museum, the dominant part of the park, the director sponsored lunch for us there and afterwards met us in the museum conference room for a press conference. Again the TV and newspaper people were there in even greater force. A very efficient translator was present. After a few preliminary remarks and questions, I was invited to read *An Open Letter to the People of Hiroshima* that I had prepared.

An open letter to the people of Hiroshima—October, 1999

I have come to Hiroshima joined by my Air Corps comrade, J. M. "Matt" Crawford as unofficial emissaries of the U.S. Air Corps 494th Bomb Group. We were both pilots of B-24 Bombers who flew missions to Japan and other Pacific locations. Matt is President of the 494th Bomb Group Veterans; I am a former POW shot down while bombing the Battleship *Haruna* in Kure Harbor and interned in Hiroshima. We are joined by my wife Carolyn and son Patrick.

Our purpose is to pay homage particularly to our friends and comrades who died here in August 1945. These included six of my bomber crew; I was spared by being transferred to Tokyo. We also come to thank and pay respect to those of you who have recognized these comrades and erected a memorial to them, especially Mr. Shigeaki Mori.

At the same time we recognize that our comrades are a few among many who died here in August 1945 and pay respect to the memory of their souls. Everyone in Hiroshima at that time was directly affected themselves or through the loss and injury of family and friends, as did many other Japanese. I am one of relatively few Americans who lost personal friends and comrades in the atomic holocaust. Perhaps this closeness aligns me more with the feelings of you, the citizens of Hiroshima. No one can know what the fate of each of us might have been if the fury of atomic fission had not been unleashed on Hiroshima. What we do know is that this force, which is so powerful that it powers the sun, and has an array of effects that even transgress generations, should never be used again to vaporize human life in wholesale and then to seep into survivors to kill or maim them, some quickly some slowly, and still to affect generations yet to be conceived. I know only the heartache—you know the heartache but also the nightmare memory and insidious residual effects.

We appreciate the reception and hospitality that has been extended to our small group—the memory of which we hope will be passed to the next generation. All of us should certainly desire to keep our family and national pride and loyalty; these are core to our human dignity and instinct. At the same time we must continue to learn how to embrace and enhance our common well being, happiness, and understanding. Whatever the results of this trip might bring I hope that it will contribute, even in an ever so small way, to continued peace and friendship.

We have learned that war brings hatred, suffering, destruction, and waste and that peace can bring happiness and prosperity. Let us teach this to our sons and daughters.

Respectfully, Thomas C. Cartwright

Matt Crawford was then invited to read the poem *Angels Weep*, written by Fred Salter, a WW II veteran who wrote this poem at the time of the controversy surrounding the placing of the *Enola Gay* in the Smithsonian Museum. His reading ended with a shaky voice and teary eyes. Verse 12, of 13, was especially appropriate for the moment:

We pray God's love spreads
    o'er the world,
And that all wars will cease.
Until that day, let's honor
    those
Who died preserving peace.

Questions followed and related mostly to my position on abolition of nuclear weapons. I made clear that any answer was a personal opinion and did in no way intend to represent the U.S. government or military. I stated that I supported banning nuclear weapons but would leave the matter of ethics of the first use of the atomic bomb and the current history revision and the Smithsonian Museum controversy to the historians. (I have stated earlier my opinion about the first uses of atomic bombs on Hiroshima and Nagasaki.)

We were given presents from the mayor of Hiroshima and the museum director, and then the director gave us a personal tour of the extensive Peace Memorial Museum. The displays depicted in vivid, gruesome detail the effects of the atomic bomb explosion and radiation on the city structure and on the people as well as the residual effects. The displays were obviously aimed at depicting the horrors resulting from the employment of a nuclear weapon. I saw no information in the museum related to the war raging at the time that the bomb was dropped—only the aftermath of the atomic bomb.

### *Taloa* Crash Site

We returned to our hotel with our hosts for a brief rest and tea. After tea we got two taxis to go to a golf course outside of the suburb of Itsukaichi-cho. At this course, constructed on steep rolling hills, a Buddhist priest, Rev. Muneo Okabe, met us and showed us where he had witnessed, as an eight-year-old, the *Taloa* crash. After taking several anti-aircraft fire hits, the *Taloa* went into a steep dive, which was terminated by half burying itself in the ground which, at that time, was terraced rice fields. Listening to this eyewitness description of the *Taloa* crashing with a reported six of our 494th mates aboard was the first of several moving accounts of witnesses. An account of the fate of the *Taloa* crew who successfully bailed out has been summarized, and more will follow about *Taloa* pilot Joe Dubinsky.

After this moving experience, we returned to our hotel after dark. By this time we were quite impressed with two young Japanese ladies who accompanied us on almost all of our trip. One was Mrs. Atsuko Shigesawa, the editor previously mentioned, and the other was Miss Akiko Naono, a Ph.D. student from the University of California at Santa Cruz doing her research in Hiroshima about survivors of the atomic bomb. They were observers but also filled in as interpreters. They both spoke excellent English (American-style) and on several occasions they cleared up translations that were, inadvertently, not correctly given to us. We invited them to dinner and they showed us to an excellent, inexpensive restaurant. We discussed the problems of translation and how memories must change over fifty-four years. We were reminded often during the next few days how memory can play tricks, influenced by time and unconscious bias. What patriot would not want his country's history to appear more favorable?

## BB *Haruna* Revisited

Mr. Mori was fatigued from the day before, so we got a later start on another fascinating day. We left Hiroshima by taxi for the suburb of Ujina, which is a port town. (Recall that this is the location where Neal and Brissette were taken by Lieutenant Fukui after the bomb was dropped—more follows.) From Ujina we caught a ferry to the Island of Etajima and along the way, the site where the *Haruna* (the battleship that we bombed) was sunk was pointed out over in Kure Bay, which we could see in the distance. After the July 28 attacks, the *Haruna* was partly exposed sitting on the floor of Kure Bay for several years before it was salvaged for scrap iron. A *Haruna* veteran suggested that the Japanese government wanted it out of sight and out of mind more than it wanted the scrap iron.

When we disembarked from the ferry on this small island with our TV crew, a newspaper reporter and cameraman, the residents, who were not used to tourists, looked on in a bit of wonderment. We again engaged taxis and proceeded across this small island to the site of a monument erected in honor of the crew of the *Haruna* who lost their lives in combat. Of the several hundred on board, "70+" crewmen were lost on July 28, 1945, when we and navy planes flying off the Ticonderoga bombed the *Haruna*.

We were met and greeted by the president of the *Haruna* veterans group, Mr. Hisahiro Mitsumine, who was most affable and informative. Another *Haruna* veteran, Mr. Takeyoshi Kondo, who had been part of a team operating an anti-aircraft position, also joined us. Our group of four stood at attention in front of the monument, bowed slightly, placed flowers at the base of the monument, and then bowed again. This ceremonial gesture was partly a TV/photo opportunity, but I believe that all of us had real feelings of compassion for the men honored by this monument who lost their lives from our bombs, who thought with fervor that they were doing the right thing just as we did.

We were gratified with this meeting and stayed around for a while discussing various things such as the direction that our planes came in from and the two 494th bombers that they shot going down in flames. Mr. Mitsumine told us a bit about the situation with the *Haruna*. This battleship had transferred all of its fuel to another battleship and was harbor-bound starting in February of 1945. This information gave Matt and me pause for reflection on the lives lost about an inoperative battleship. Matt was not on the *Haruna* mission but a few days before had flown a dangerous weather reconnaissance mission just outside Kure Bay. An almost instant camaraderie was established between Mr. Mitsumine, Matt, and me. We exchanged small talk and got a big laugh out of my observation that they were very accurate anti-aircraft gunners—something that I had known for fifty-four years and did not think I would ever laugh about. This experience of meeting two men who had been as close as "face to face" as possible with enemies between a battleship and a bomber was indeed an emotional experience. It left me pondering how we had become enemies intent on killing each other.

After having lived most of our productive life and having had many years to reflect, and perhaps mellow, we could now look on the experience from a different, more humane, and civilized perspective. We were beginning to feel, I believe, that the Japanese that we had met were very grateful for two involved as veterans coming in peace and sharing this with a son; a point emphasized in Japanese culture is stated as "passing from son to son."

We returned to the ferry and sailed back to Ujina. There Mr. Mori took us to the place where Japanese Military Police Lieutenant Fukui had taken Neal and Brissette, along with a captured B-29 crew, to a military post where he thought that they would be safe from being killed by revengeful military or civilians. (Refer to the earlier section on Ralph Neal.) The old military post buildings and prison were long gone and were now replaced by a very nicely landscaped parking lot for office buildings. We placed flowers there in memory of these two men who had endured unimaginable suffering from "radiation sickness" and died August 19, 1945. The rescue of the B-29 crew by Lieutenant Fukui and the suffering of Neal and Brissette is best described by Lt. Walter Ross, bombardier of the B-29, in his book *Courage Beyond the Blindfold.* A reporter asked me what my feelings were when we placed a wreath at the site of Neal and Brissette's deaths. Respectfully placing a wreath to signify that we have not forgotten them and holding their memory and their families' loss in our minds forever was all we could do—there is no way to adequately put into words feelings at such an emotional experience.

The next day we had prepared to leave Hiroshima and were waiting in the rather large hotel lobby where Mrs. Mori and others had come to see us off. Carolyn was standing a bit apart from the men, and Mrs. Mori walked up to her and said, "I have a present for you," and then very quietly sang close to Carolyn's ear a Japanese song about birds and butterflies. She is a vocalist and sang beautifully in this intimate way that was very touching for Carolyn. This type of intimate present may be customary in Japan or it may have been a unique idea of Mrs. Mori, a very gracious person, but it was a touching experience that Carolyn will never forget.

### Memories Revisited

We left Hiroshima by train with Mr. Mori, Atsuko, and the TV crew for Otake, which was to the south and west. From there we would begin our tour to the sites where we had parachuted, were captured, and the *Lonesome Lady* crashed into a rice paddy. Mr. Keiichi Muranaka, our host, met us at the train station along with his son-in-law, Mr. Kazuo Muranaka, who was our chauffeur, and his cousin, Mr. Masazo Asatsui, sixty-eight years old, who had been in the Military Police in Hiroshima but was not in Hiroshima on the day of the atomic bombing. He had helped the U.S. Army research the remains of American fliers who were killed in Hiroshima and after the war worked at the Iwakuni U.S. Marine base and was our translator along with help from Atsuko. We traveled together in an excellent Toyota van. The TV crew followed in their van.

Mr. Muranaka was a superb host and made our day most eventful. He wanted us to see where he had been trained as an anti-aircraft gunner after bring drafted in April of 1945. However, the battleship *Ise* to which he was assigned was sunk on a July 24, 1945, raid while in Kure Harbor as he waited at an anti-aircraft battery on shore to be sent aboard. Next we went to the Iwakuni U.S. Marine Base where Major Keefe met us and hosted us to a nice coffee and discussion about our trip. He was very supportive of Mr. Mori's activities and our reinforcement of them. Major Keefe represented the U.S. at the dedication of the memorial plaque Mr. Mori erected in Hiroshima when the U.S. Consulate refused an invitation. We were all proud to be represented by Major Keefe, a marine of impressive physical stature, clean-cut, straightforward, and dedicated to promoting peaceful relations. He complimented our small party for coming to Japan and meeting with the people. Our mission was not planned as a peace mission, but Major Keefe told us that this sort of contact was very effective in promoting good relations with the Japanese people.

After leaving the marine base, we were hosted to a delightful lunch at a picturesque traditional Japanese restaurant nestled in a setting by a beautiful waterfall. From there we traveled on smaller and smaller roads through scenic, forest-covered hills and cultivated valleys. As the population became more sparse, we were enjoying the scenery and were not prepared for the emotional experiences just ahead of us.

## Memories Expanded

We arrived at a typical farm house, though more rambling than usual, overlooking fields of rice and other crops in a valley. After finding the lady living there alone, our host introduced us to Mrs. Mika Marumo. She appeared to be about our age and presumably had been informed about our coming visit but was nevertheless overwhelmed by the crowd and TV people who were filming every step. She bowed deeply and sunk to the floor, sitting on her heels in apparent dismay. After some polite con-versation she relaxed some and told her story of hearing an air-plane and seeing it fly by, trailing smoke, and then a parachute falling into the field about 200 meters away into a field in front of her house. The "soldier" was soon "surrounded by village people." Her father, who had lost a son in the war as a kamikaze pilot, picked up his rifle (which was illegally kept) and headed toward the American enemy who had landed in his field. As de-scribed in the booklet by Mrs. Teruko Fujinaka, "Genji Marumo-san tried to shoot the soldier with a rifle to fulfill his enmity of his son being killed in the war; however, he himself was shot." When I had read this earlier, I had assumed that he had been shot by some Japanese authority and was not killed, but his daughter told the story in full detail. Apparently the "soldier" (one of my crew) thought, correctly, that he was going to be shot himself, so he shot and killed her father in self-defense. I re-viewed the story with Atsuko to be sure that the translation was correct, and she affirmed that I understood it correctly. Mr. Mori wrote me later that he had withheld telling me this part of the story and apologized if it caused me unpleasant feelings.

This humble lady was not hostile and wanted to be a good hostess. She took us into her house and showed us her Buddhist shrine where the names of her father, brother, and other de-ceased relatives were inscribed on wooden pieces, as is custom-ary, and kept on a special rack. She demonstrated taking these name plates out of the rack and placing them on the shrine for prayers. At this time we presented flowers to her by placing the arrangement at the altar. We had gone back outside and were preparing to leave after apologizing to her for our intrusion and thanking her for telling us about the "soldier" and her father. She said something and ran back into her house and came out with some yen that she had and offered it to us, apologizing for not having a proper present for visitors.

After returning to the U.S., I wrote Mrs. Marumo to thank her for receiving us and for telling us about her experiences, and I asked Mr. Mori to have it translated and sent to her. Instead he had the letter translated and took it to her in person. Edited, it read :

Dear Mrs. Marumo,

You may recall that I visited your home in October along with my wife and son. A TV crew, a newspaper reporter, and others were also with us. First, my apologies for intruding on your home with so many people. You were a very gracious hostess to us and we appreciate that very much.

You told us the story of one of my B-24 bomber crew coming down by parachute in the field in front of your house. It was the first time that I learned that this soldier, an enemy in your country, shot your father. Your father's son, your brother, being killed in the war and then your father himself being killed was a great tragedy of war. Although I do not know the circumstances, I can imagine the great grief and hardships that these losses were to you and your family.

This soldier who parachuted was later himself killed by the atomic bomb. I do not know which of my crew this soldier was, but he was one of my crew and a friend. Also, five others of my bomber crew were killed in Hiroshima. Because I share the grief of Hiroshima with all Japanese, I came to Japan to share my feeling that these terrible things are caused by war. We now live in peace and we enjoy the benefits of friendship and prosperity. Let us not forget the horrors of war and learn to live in peace and be willing to help one another and be friends.

My wife, my son, and I will never forget your hospitality in inviting us into your home and sharing your personal shrine with us. It was a privilege to be allowed to place flowers at this shrine in memory of your deceased family. We are grateful to have had the opportunity to meet you and extend to you our very best wishes for health and happiness.

Mrs. Marumo wrote back:

Dear Dr. Cartwright,

I am Mika Marumo. You were visited with a flower to my house in the late Fall [1999]. I was very glad to see you. When you were visited you offered a flower in my Budhist [sic] altar I expressed my joy heartily. I didn't bear a grudge against the American. It was my honest feeling. Today you gave me the letter made to be impressed deeply. Mr. Mori read it aloud in Japanese. Tears appeared in my eyes hearing it. Father of the heaven is glad at your letter too. It was guided to the tomb of the father buried in the public cemetery after that with Mr. Mori. When Father died he was 53 years old. Father loved me very much. I liked him too. Again it appreciates you. Thank you very much.

Later Mr. Mori traveled again to see her and present flowers to cheer her up as she was despondent because she lost her husband and now had no family. Mr. Mori read my second letter to her, and she asked him to send her brief answer:

Dear Dr. Cartwright,
   I don't hate an American. Father should run away early from the enemy who had a pistol. I offered your letter in the Buddhist family alter. Then I prayed the mercy of late Mr. Genji Marumo [her father].

How could I not feel for this lady and at the same time feel for the unimaginable trauma my friend, one of my crew, who had been under my command, had experienced? His ordeal included flying through a flak field, riding a gyrating plane on fire, bailing out, being surrounded by the enemy, being threatened by an enraged farmer, having to kill a person, and who knows what else. However, he somehow surrendered or was captured. There was an interpreter present and the soldier was taken to a local prison. It is a wonder that he survived that long. Either he used his sidearm to hold the local people at bay, or perhaps even though possibly being in a mob mood, these farmers respected human life and civilized procedures and properly turned him into authorities. As with all of my crew, except Abel and Pedersen, he was taken to Hiroshima from a local prison. We learned later that he was scheduled to be shipped out to Tokyo on August 7 (the day after the bomb) for trial for murder.

While trying to cope with imagining how the capture and shooting occurred and which of my buddies this could have been, and sorting out what to believe and what I could question, we loaded in the van for the next stop. After reflection and taking other sources into account, I believe that the above account is correct.

Next we stopped in front of another more rambling than usual farm house; it occurred to me that it was probably, at least at one time, where an extended family lived. A rather stout farmer, Mr. Masatoshi Fujioka, who was wearing rubber boots, came up out of the field where he had been tending his rice field. After a few preliminaries, he began describing his sighting of the smoking *Lonesome Lady* flying in an arc on its way to crash a few kilometers away. He observed from in front of his house several, perhaps four, parachutes coming down, but being a boy of nine years he was kept at his house and could not explore further. This event apparently was a highlight of his youth, which he seemed to remember very vividly.

Four of the crew came down in the area in front of the farmer boy's house that was not visible to him. The landing and capture of all four are recorded in the booklet *The Fallen B-24* by Mrs. Teruko Fujinaka as described by eyewitness accounts. One came down near the village of Gantoku Line and for some reason he got on a train and tried to communicate with a high school girl using an English/Japanese dictionary. He was probably trying to convey the message "take me to a military base or military person," but he was "captured" at the next station. Another two came down close to Kino and were captured by villagers. One lady whose son was killed in the war tried to "hit them." Another came down in front of Mr. Hirai's house near Nikenbiraki. His heel was "shot" and he could not walk. Mr. Hirai's sister, who was a nurse, "took care of his wound." This soldier and the two from Kino were put in a car and driven to the Takamori Police Station.

These four and the one who shot the enraged farmer are not identified by name in any record that has surfaced. The one with the "shot" heel was probably Jim Ryan, judging from reports from Hiroshima. It is significant to note, I believe, that even though there was understandable hostility against these four of my crew, they were not beheaded or beaten to death and, judging from the fact that a man took three of them in his car to a police station, there was obviously respect for civil procedures and somehow minimal mutual trust existed.

At the next stop of our caravan we met a lady, Mrs. Sumiko Fujinaka, and her husband at the village of Amagane. The husband had been off to war in the Pacific when his wife had seen my parachute come down and sometime later me walking out with Mr. Seiichi Tamai. We walked a short distance from her home, and she pointed out the spot several hundred meters away where she remembered me landing. I had recollections of coming down in a clearing with trees on all sides so that no houses were in sight and was a bit perplexed, thinking maybe she had observed Copilot Looper instead of me. I was skeptical of her story, but my wife pointed out that trees could have been cleared during the past fifty-four years.

I asked where the plane came down, and the husband pointed and said 1,000 meters in that direction. I must have bailed out at a lower altitude than I thought because my plane in a steep dive traveled only about a kilometer before crashing. Looper came down in a field at a place not far away called Mitagahara and was taken by Koreans working there. We were both taken to the Ikachi Police Station and then transferred to a police station in the city of Yanai before being taken to Hiroshima. I now feel sure that these people had the story correct and my memory just needed some prompting.

### Dream Never Dreamed

As we settled back in the van to move on, the four of us had been exposed to a lot of new information, talked to several eyewitnesses, and were trying to figure out just what happened to whom and were having many recollections about our crew and their fate. My thoughts were consumed by the events that seemed to have been flashing by too quickly. We had hardly settled in the van when it pulled around a small community center building and the door slid open to a crowd of about seventy people standing and clapping in front of a huge sign behind them reading "WELCOME DR. CARTWRIGHT to Ikachi." We were overwhelmed and nearly speechless. We were introduced to some of the principals and a few politicians present and shown the monument in front of the community center that they had erected to recognize our crew.

We then trekked a few hundred meters to the site of the crash of the *Lonesome Lady*. Several people who had witnessed the errant plane coming down in a sweeping arc described in some detail the path of descent and crash in a rice paddy. Apparently, one propeller had come off and crashed through a farm house, setting it afire. One engine broke lose and catapulted some distance. The wings broke into two pieces and each was blown to the next paddies. One fellow recovered the life raft and used it for years. Apparently, much of the aluminum wings and fuselage tore up into parts. The school girls (all the boys were either recruited into the military or worked in war material plants) were assigned to carry all the parts that they could down to the place where the community center now stands. Since all household utensils that were metal had been sent to the war effort, the people garnered parts of the wreckage and made frying pans, winnow pans for separating their rice, dust pans, etc. A few years ago they sent several of these handmade tools to me in a goodwill gesture. One is placed in a military museum on the campus of Texas A&M University, where I was a professor.

On the walk up to see the crash area and back, several of the eyewitnesses were anxious to talk to me and described their experience about seeing the crash and the reaction of the community. This was an isolated agricultural community and no air raids or close flyover had occurred, so our "landing" there was a big event.

As described above, Navigator Roy Pedersen's parachute did not open and he fell to the ground in a pine forest not too far away. His body was not found until two years later, when the forest was clear cut. This fact illustrates the isolation of this area in a country where there is not much vacant land. The steep hills are all pine forests and only the valleys are cultivated.

Back from the crash site to the community center and monument, where chairs and tables were set up, the crowd gathered around. Mr. Muranaka made formal introductions of a number of people including the families who had sent pieces of the *Lonesome Lady* to me and the ones who had been most instrumental in having the monument erected. He continued with introductory remarks and asked me to respond, which I did by reading my open letter to the people of Ikachi area.

An Open Letter to the People of Ikachi Area—October, 1999
My name is Tom Cartwright and I was the Pilot of the *Lonesome Lady*, a U.S. B-24 Bomber that crashed near your village on July 28, 1945. Having parachuted before the crash, I along with my copilot Lt. Durden Looper, were taken prisoners of war here. I am privileged to be welcomed back to your village. Could

anyone have imagined in 1945 my returning here, welcomed in peace? I am pleased to be accompanied by Mr. Matt Crawford, President of our B-24 Bombardment Group Veterans, my wife Carolyn, my son Dr. Pat Cartwright.

You may not be aware that, in retrospect, I feel fortunate that on our fateful mission, after our plane was damaged beyond continued flight, it brought us to your community. We were at war with one another and we represented your enemy. Except for our Navigator, Lt. Roy Pedersen, whose parachute failed to open, our entire crew survived heavy anti-aircraft fire, parachuting out of a burning plane, and being captured in enemy territory. We were not welcome guests, but one injured airman's wounds were treated and none of us was seriously maltreated. I am fortunate that the *Lonesome Lady*, damaged and uncontrollable, flew toward this area and maintained sufficient altitude for me to bail out in your community. After I retired the one thing that I most wanted to do was to return to this village.

I wanted to return because of a longing deep in my heart to see the crash site and where I was captured. But much more than curiosity I wanted to come here to thank those of you who sent me parts of the *Lonesome Lady* as good will gestures. And then I was overwhelmed to learn that you erected the monument as a memorial to those killed in the war and specifically recognized "the dreadful accident" of the *Lonesome Lady* listing the seven airmen of her crew who died and stating that "These soldiers gave their lives for their country."

The character of this community is embodied, I believe, in the above and in the following inscriptions on the monument:

> Appreciating today's peace we erect this monument.
> We heartily hope that happiness will continue forever,
> from father to son, from son to son.

I am especially pleased that my son asked to join us so that, as the inscription admonishes, the next generations will take notice and remember.

We are honored to be your guests which gives us a chance to meet you, thank you in person and to pay homage to our fallen comrades at this most appropriate place by your historic monument.

Respectfully, Thomas C. Cartwright

After a few questions and comments, I asked to read my letter to Mr. Muranaka.

Dear Mr. Muranaka,

There are several things that I never dreamed would happen to me:

Having a piece of the *Lonesome Lady* mounted on a plaque in my house.

Returning to the village where the *Lonesome Lady* crashed and I was captured.

Having a monument erected honoring the souls of my fallen comrades.

Corresponding with friends in the Yanai area.

Meeting you in person and shaking your hand.

These dreams began to come true when I received your first letter in 1985. I am forever grateful to you for your thoughtful letters and kind acts to me. I shall cherish your letter which accompanied a piece of our crashed B-24 Bomber which you gave to me. It said: "Now I would like to give you this article which I have kept all these years as a reminder of the sad experiences we shared during that terrible time in history. By remembering we shall be able to maintain this peace we know now. This is our responsibility."

I mounted this piece on a plaque and inscribed your words above on it. I added "This memento is dedicated to the memory of those of the *Lonesome Lady* crew who perished in and around Hiroshima. Mr. Muranaka's return of this fragment is gratefully appreciated and was accepted and preserved in the spirit of peace that he stated—it is much more than a twisted piece of a crashed bomber—it is a symbol of both our regrets and our hopes."

My first encounter with Japan was hostile and terrifying. My second encounter in 1983, to attend a technical conference, was pleasant but a short trip to Hiroshima was almost unbearable emotionally. Now my third trip, though still grieving for my fallen comrades, I am glad that I came and feel that I am among friends who share my grief as well as my hopes for lasting peace and prosperity.

With gratitude and respect,

Tom Cartwright

These statements seemed to be well received. After the talks, Japanese tea was served to the guests in formal style, which included elaborate preparation and serving in traditional attire. Afterwards, we began to mix with the crowd and talk to individuals. We were presented with beautiful flowers and a number of presents. I was impressed by a very elegant-looking lady who came up to me and spoke in English and introduced herself as Mrs. Takako Yorimoto. She explained to me that her family had contributed the natural stone and polished granite plates which held the inscriptions of the monument. She gave us a very nice carved granite turtle which has a place in Japanese tradition. The lady who wrote the booklet *The Fallen B-24,* Mrs. Teruko Fujinaka, introduced herself and appeared very gracious in her welcome to us. She had been instrumental in getting the community behind supporting the erection of the monument. Her son and husband were also present and visited with us and wanted to have their pictures taken with us.

### Unexpected Meetings

Ms. Fukui, daughter of Lieutenant Fukui, introduced herself, much to my surprise, having come some distance to Ikachi. She gave me a copy of some of Lieutenant Fukui's personal diary in which he wrote about the B-29 crew that he had rescued and about picking up Neal and Brissette in Hiroshima. Everything in the diary is confirmed by Lieutenant Ross in his book *Courage Beyond the Blindfold.* Also included in the diary were some reflections that Lieutenant Fukui had written in 1983 and are copied in part below.

> Our Lord creat the earth and educates people to maintain eternal peace but if special governors betrayed God Will, worsest earth will shurely be realized.
>
> To-day attached description [a newspaper article revealing that U.S. airmen were killed by the atomic bomb in Hiroshima] should be carefully read and atomic bomb explusion killed twenty three [later corrected but the number is still in question] in Hiroshima. U.S. goverment should correct her wrong history as quick as possible and U.S. gov. should favour them with highest fame changing unknown death.

A lady who signed her name as T. Nakashiba came up and talked to me, speaking English quite well. She graciously welcomed me to Ikachi and said that meeting me was an unexpected pleasure. As she left she handed me something that she had written while sitting at this meeting, which I thought was interesting.

> It was hot in Summer vacation afternoon. I felt like war was coming to an end even ones child heart. Sudenly one bomber crashing under fire and disappeard western over the hill. What happened! cried my mother. I saw that moment when I was 6 years old. I never forgot that moment, but you still alive in front of me I cant believe.
>
> In those days we ate grass and leaves of trees. After a while Japan was defeated by the United states. There was a lot of different cind of sacrifice each other [for both sides].
>
> I am thinking if we had been defeated by the U.S.S.R. we would not live.
>
> Thank you the United States finally. We pray the partnership between the U.S. and Japan will last forever.

Matt, Pat, and Carolyn also talked with various people as interpreters were available. Carolyn in her way went around and shook hands and hugged all of the ladies. When we got in the van to leave, these ladies, who were mostly from local farm families, pressed around the van smiling and waving, focusing on Carolyn, who had to wipe a tear away. We drove through the village of Ikachi to see the site of the police station where I was taken from Ikachi. From there we had a nice scenic drive back to Mr. Muranaka's present home city of Yanai. During this trip we noted that the clean roadsides added to the attractiveness of the country side.

## Winding Down

We were met at our hotel in Yanai by Mrs. Muranaka and her daughter, who hosted us for a late afternoon tea and presented us with presents. We presented flowers to Mrs. Muranaka and her daughter. The next morning they, including a grandson, all met us to take us to the train station and see us off to Hiroshima. Mr. Muranaka traveled back with us to Hiroshima to make sure that we were comfortable and made our connections. We could not imagine more friendly and hospitable people. Even though the Muranakas and the Moris were exceptional hosts, all of the limited sample of Japanese people that we met were considerate, polite, and welcomed us.

We boarded the train to Hiroshima but only to transfer there to go on to the historic city of Kyoto as tourists for parts of three days. The TV crew had ended their filming at Ikachi, and we were surprised to see them greet us as we stepped off the train in Hiroshima to transfer to the bullet train to Kyoto. The NHK producer, Deyama, and the interpreter, Miwako, were there but with no cameras. They knew our schedule and only wanted to take us through the several floors and many platforms of the train station to the correct train. So with these two and Mr. Muranaka we found our way to the correct place—only numbers were decipherable to us as other parts of signs were in Japanese, so we really appreciated being guided and helped with baggage. We were a few minutes early and as a train pulled in to our platform we were told that it was not ours—the next one was listed in the schedule as the one that we wanted.

These trains run on schedule almost to the second, but we boarded the next train to pull in without looking at our watches. Deyama took us on board as the schedule called for a seven-minute stop. When we arrived at our reserved seats, a very nicely dressed lady was sitting there and Deyama politely asked if she was in the correct seat. She pulled out her stub without smiling and showed that she was indeed in her assigned seat. Deyama looked at our stubs and they listed the same seat for one of us. The lady reached over and took our stubs and told Deyama that we were on the wrong train. At that time the train pulled out of the station and Deyama's mouth dropped open in disbelief. The lady explained that this was a special train that ran only two months of the year, three days a week to accommodate the extra traffic traveling to see the fall leaves turning and was not on the printed schedule. This lady, whom we thought at first to be very haughty, turned out to be very friendly and helpful. She told us in perfect "American" that this train was headed for Kyoto so not to worry. Deyama also announced not to worry, he would find the "driver" of the train and straighten everything out and then jump off at the next station and catch the first train back to Hiroshima. He did all of this, and the lady came up to our newly assigned seats and sat and talked with us. She was a medical doctor, and Pat and she went back to her seat and talked about medical practices in Japan and America.

## Added Meeting

After all other arrangements had been made for us, Mr. Mori scheduled one last meeting with three men for the evening of the day that we arrived at our hotel in Kyoto. We learned a lot from these men about history of direct interest to us, as I am sure Mr. Mori knew we would. Also, I am sure that it was difficult to arrange for these three men to travel to a meeting point. Pat had gone to give a lecture at the Nagoya Medical College the next day, so Matt, Carolyn, and I met with them. Mr. Mori came to Kyoto for the meeting in order to introduce us.

One of the three men, Mr. Kazushi Higashida, is director of the Japanese CEO Organization, and a spokesman for Japanese business. Another was Dr. Akio Nakamura, a retired professor of agriculture, whose father was a colonel at the Chugoku Military Police Headquarters and was in charge of my crew while we were imprisoned there. The third was Mr. Toru Fukubayashi, a teacher and historian characterized as the person most knowledgeable about allied planes shot down over Japan and the fate of their crews. An American, Mr. Barry Keith, a Ph.D. student at the University of Kyoto, was our interpreter and a very good one. A lady reporter was also present.

Mr. Higashida was the first to present a statement. He had been a cadet at the Chugoku Military Police Headquarters and had been assigned the duty on August 5, 1945, of interrogating a POW whom he identified as Lieutenant Dubinsky. Although there was some conflicting evidence, the official U.S. records reported that Dubinsky had died when he had bailed out of the falling *Taloa* too late for his chute to open. Mr. Higashida went into detail about Dubinsky pulling a picture of his girlfriend out of his flight suit pocket to show him. Also he showed him a locket that he pulled out of another pocket on the leg of his flight suit; his girlfriend had given him this as a good luck charm. During the interrogation they discussed the fact that they were both economics students and were drafted at the same age. Through this meeting Mr. Higashida developed a liking for Dubinsky and asked him if there was anything he could do to make him more comfortable. Dubinsky mentioned being plagued by mosquitoes, so Cadet Higashida ordered that the POWs be given mosquito coils. His statements were obviously aimed at convincing us that Dubinsky had survived bailing out and capture but was killed by the atomic bomb.

I thought that it was highly unlikely that Dubinsky would have been allowed to keep on his person a picture and a locket, based on my experience. Therefore, I remained skeptical, thinking that it could have been a case of mistaken identity even though Mr. Higashida was very insistent that it was Dubinsky. After reading about my doubts, Mr. Fukubayashi has stated that "It is very likely that Dubinsky was captured alive, because there are some eyewitnesses who say 3 fliers being captured near the crash site of the *Taloa*. Mr. Mori was told by an eyewitness (a Kempei Tai man [Secret Police]) that 'the third flier had been found unconscious hanging on the tree. He later recovered consciousness and was sent to Hiroshima.'" The conflicts that have become evident in the oral and written history about Dubinsky's fate illustrate the problems of determining correct history long after the fact. Knowing the thoroughness and dedication of Mr. Mori and Mr. Fukubayashi, I believe that Lieutenant Dubinsky survived bailing out of the *Taloa* and was interned in Hiroshima as they indicate, and may well have perished from effects of the atomic bomb rather than from bailing out too late.

The next day after his interrogation of Dubinsky, Mr. Higashida reported that he was in his barracks when the atomic bomb was dropped. Of the fifty-three men in that building, only three survived the atomic explosion which caused the collapsing and shattering of the barracks. Of those three, two died within a year and only he lived. He talked for about an hour and then got up, shook hands, and left. The next day the Kyoto paper reported our meeting but never mentioned Mr. Higashida by name—he was referred to only as an Osaka businessman who was a veteran. We presumed that he had requested anonymity.

Mr. Akio Nakamura next explained that his father, a colonel, was commander of the Chugoku Military Police Headquarters and was in charge of prisoners there. Col. Shigeo Nakamura had witnessed the *Taloa* going down. On August 4 he had complained that they were getting too crowded with POWs and wanted to send some away. Akio became curious as a thirteen-year-old and wanted to see Americans—especially American POWs. His father let him go with him into three cells while he examined three POWs. Akio, as a boy, had drawn sketches of them and later tried to identify them from a picture of our crew. He thought one was Atkinson, who was sitting on the floor and was not well. He identified one who was lying on a pallet with an injured foot as Looper (I believe that it was more likely Ryan). The third was likely Porter, reported to be standing and looking somewhat defiant.

Mr. Nakamura further explained that his father is the one who interrogated me in Hiroshima and decided that I was one who should be sent to Tokyo for further interrogation. One officer and two military guards, I believe, accompanied me and two navy POWs on the trip to Tokyo. During a transfer of trains in Osaka, a mob spotted us and wanted to kill us. One of our two guards was injured by rocks thrown at us, but they managed to get us onto the train before the incident could escalate further. I was aware of a hostile crowd gathering at some train station but, being blindfolded, I had no idea where it was or that it could have become serious. Mr. Nakamura has written this story and given me a translated copy, which includes his sketch of the three POWs that he observed. Listening over that week to eye-witnesses whose lives came within a few meters crossing the path of my life, I learned new things and recalled old memories. Mr. Nakamura added significant items to my store of memories.

Mr. Mori then turned to Mr. Toru Fukubayashi, informing us that he was a historian who had assembled the most complete records about allied airmen who had been shot down over Japan and of their fate. Mr. Fukubayashi presented us with a written account, in English, of all planes downed over Japan on July 28, 1945 (the date we went down) in the Chugoku-Shikoku District (the district where we went down). Also attached to this report was a most interesting map and chart dividing Japan into seven regions and summarizing for each region the number of planes of the U.S. and allied countries that went down in that region during the war. Also listed were the number of airmen who died in crashes and the number captured. Of those captured he listed the number who died of disease or injury, were executed or murdered, died in air raids, including the fire storms of Tokyo and atomic bombing of Hiroshima, and finally the number who lived and were repatriated. Almost all of these were, of course, Americans and were returned to the U.S.

I turned to the page where he had listed: "B-24 (No. 44-40680, nickname LONESOME LADY from Okinawa Air Base)." A nearly full-page account of where I was captured, held, etc., was given. It was completely accurate as far as I could tell. I am sure that he had gotten much information from local history buffs such as Mr. Mori. The speaker at the 494th Reunion in Salt Lake City emphasized that it is important to record the details of history; Mr. Fukubayashi has done a real service for all of us and for the historical record.

After our meeting Matt, Carolyn, and I were treated by our three remaining hosts to a delightful dinner. This was a memorable way to end our visit to pay tribute to our fallen comrades and learn more of our history.

### Reflected Reflections

We now felt that our hosts along with many others that we met were truly our friends. We left Japan with the feeling that the past week had been one of the most memorable times of our lives. I had come to Japan twice before—once as a POW and once as a professional without acquaintances or friends—and left each of those two times as a foreigner feeling that I had intruded and did not share common ideals. This time, with hosts who had been established as friends through much correspondence, I felt comfortable about coping with memories confronted at Hiroshima. By the time we left, I felt not only that I had made more friends, but that I had adopted a mission that was very much in evidence in the people of Hiroshima: that of the abolition of nuclear weapons. This mission, the purpose of which I believe is shared by the majority of Americans, is a worldwide issue.

Our itinerary included only Japanese who were friendly. We are under no delusion that there are those who hold resentments and perhaps even hostility toward the U.S.; however, we did not meet anyone who expressed these attitudes. The documentary made by NHK TV was entitled *Gekitsui No Chie* and subtitled *Moto Beigunkicho 55 Nen Me NO Nippon,* which may be translated as *Coming to the Land Where the Plane Crashed,* subtitled *The Former Air Force Pilot Visiting Japan 55 Years Later.* The fact that this program was shown twice in the Hiroshima area and then shown nationally was an indication of interest.

Several things in our limited observations impressed us about the people and the country. One was that they seemed genuinely appreciative of their treatment by the United States after the war. Another was the general politeness of the people and the cleanliness of everything. The taxis were immaculate, and the roadsides were clean. Sure, Japan has at times exploited the advantages that the U.S. made possible after the war and has become wealthy, perhaps in a way simply attempting to emulate the example of the U.S. Sure, there is denial of atrocities and failure to teach realistic history of Japan's role in the war, but it was evident that there are those who believe that the correct history should be recorded and taught. These are the people that we met and we count as friends.

# EPILOGUE

The return to Japan was immensely satisfying to me, and I believe to Carolyn, Pat, and Matt. I now believe that I know most of the major events of the history of my crew and me in Japan in 1945 and feel that void gone, but to me there is no such thing as closure, whatever that means. I do have much better feelings about the Japanese people, at least the ones that we met, and their desire for lasting peace and their appreciation for the U.S. giving them a chance to recover from a devastating war. The historical novel *Riding the East Wind* by a well-known Japanese author, O. Kaga, has recently been translated and published in English. I believe this book portrays the varied feelings of Japanese people before and during WW II and the frenzy induced by this war.

Although we did not meet any Japanese who were openly hostile to us as victors coming to Japan to open old wartime memories, there are probably Japanese who hold those feelings. Also, even though our small group came in peace with an open mind, there are Americans, especially those who were badly mistreated and brutalized, and the families of POWs who were executed, who will never forgive the Japanese for their atrocities. I do not presume to suggest that these people should be forgiving or attempt to convert them. I can only wish that they could meet Mr. Mori and Mr. Muranaka and their families as well as Atsuko, Akiko, Mrs. Fujinaka, Mrs. Marumo, Major Keefe, and all the others that we met in Japan. Perhaps such meetings would convince them that the actions of those who perpetrated the horrors that they experienced, and whose effects are still ingrained, were exacerbated by the frenzy of war time and their actions are not a characteristic inherent in all Japanese people.

My return to memories in Japan, along with much new information and recollections reinforced, even though satisfying in many ways, disheartened me about two events that loom large in my feelings. Some may dismiss these events as just part of wartime happenings. One was the failure of our highest officials, even up to our commander in chief, for not reporting, recognizing, or, if you please, admitting that American POWs were in Hiroshima and killed by our atomic bomb. This was a signal event in history that sacrificed Americans who should not have been ignored. I believe that the families of those POWs killed in Hiroshima would reinforce this feeling. This negligence, or cover-up for whatever the reason, left these families living in anxiety for too long. Also it deprived these loyal airmen and their families from being acknowledged for their ultimate sacrifice at a time that would have been most appropriate. In addition it is a disservice to the American people. We like to think we can be proud as Americans of the honesty and fairness of our country.

Another event that I resent is that of the high officials conducting the war in the Pacific, especially those ordering air strikes as the war was nearing an end. Knowing that the Japanese Naval Fleet anchored and stuck in the Japanese Inland Sea was no longer mobile, they continued to order the Air Force and Navy to bomb these targets known for extremely heavy anti-aircraft capabilities from both anchored ships and shore installations. Also our Bombardment Group only had bombs that were inadequate for sinking capital warships. These ships were harbor bound and had been for some time. The incentive for ordering missions to attack these targets, which were known to be costly of lives, appears, from the evidence, to have been based more on the egos of commanding officers than on strategically important purposes. This conclusion is reinforced by others such as in the book *The Army Air Forces In World War II* by W. F. Cravens and J. F. Cate, which states (Vol. 5, page 698): "On July 28, [1945] in a mission understandable only as a competition with the Third Fleet, which had attacked the targets on [July] the 24th [1945] and was again attacking them that day, 79 FEAF B-24s attempted to bomb Japanese capital ships anchored at Kure. . . . Most of the vessels had been hopelessly damaged, but their crews put up a 'most terrific curtain of flak'." Another book, *The Fast Carriers*, C. G. Reynolds, states that ". . . the fast carriers launched their last strike of the war against the immobile (Japanese) Mobile Fleet on 24 and 28 July, 1945 . . . an action, incidentally, Admiral Cain considered a waste of time. Joined by AAF B-24s, the carrier planes severely damaged several capital ships at Kure, some of which sank until they settled on the shallow bottom. Halsey could rest now that the *Ise* and *Hyuga,* which had escaped him at Leyte and the South China Sea sweep, were among those bottomed, as was the battleship *Haruna*."

My entire crew was always loyal and obedient and honored all orders given to us from those in charge. Our time in combat was limited, but we never flinched and carried out our orders to the best of our ability without question. I now feel that our loyalty was betrayed as the quotations above illustrate. This, again, was a disservice to all those killed and maimed. As well, these imperious actions belied the traditional American respect for life. Even so, there is no question that our military leadership was the best in the world, and for this I give thanks and readily recognize.

During the return trip to Japan, reporters and commentators would often ask me, for example, while standing beside a memorial plaque dedicated to my comrades and just after seeing it for the first time and placing flowers there, "What are your feelings now?" There was no way to express feelings hoarded for fifty-five years while memories came cascading into my mind. I would try to say something appropriate, but would always feel that it was inadequate. Now trying to put into words and summarizing about "how I feel now" about going back one last time to Hiroshima, I feel inadequate again. I had never dreamed that I would have close friends, admired friends, in Hiroshima with whom I would correspond and share thoughts; that I would see the places where we parachuted and the *Lonesome Lady* crashed; that the people in the villages who captured us would welcome me back in grand fashion. And many more things. Perhaps the best summary is to say that good dreams now linger with me more than the nightmares of the past.

# APPENDIX

A memorial tablet entitled "In honor and memory of the U.S. Army Air Force and U.S. Navy airmen who lost their lives while prisoners of war at Hiroshima, Japan, the day of the bomb—August 6, 1945," was dedicated August 5, 1989, at the Andersonville National Historic Site and National POW-MIA Museum, Andersonville, Georgia. Nine POWs are listed by name including six of my crew. President Reagan, President Carter, and Senator Sam Nunn sent messages read at the dedication. A brief historical summary about these POWs was prepared for the dedication ceremony. This historical summary, which contains some inaccuracies, is given below.

THE STORY OF THE AMERICAN POWS AT HIROSHIMA

An American Navy Helldiver bomber was part of a mission launched from the aircraft carrier, U.S.S. *Ticonderoga*, on July 28, 1945, to attack the Japanese cruiser *Tone*, which had taken refuge in Kure Harbor, Japan, a major Japanese naval center.

During the attack the Navy bomber was hit by enemy ground fire and crashed in the Inland Japanese Sea, where its two crewmen, Lt/JG. Raymond G. Porter of Butler, Pa., the pilot, and A/3C

95

Normand Rolland Brissette of Lowell, Mass., the rear gunner/radio operator, were captured by Japanese forces. They were taken to the city of Hiroshima for imprisonment and interrogation.

Also on July 28, two U.S. Army Air Corps' B-24 Liberator Bombers were part of a mission that took off from Okinawa to also attack targets in Kure Harbor, particularly the Japanese fast battleship *Haruna*, one of the last surviving Japanese battleships of the war in the Pacific.

After dropping their bombs, the two Liberators, in order to avoid heavy Japanese anti-aircraft fire, flew over Hiroshima. Both were hit by Japanese ground fire from a battery located within the city.

One of the Liberators, the *Taloa*, had eleven men aboard, including ten crewmen and an observer. Only five men survived the crash. Of these five, two were killed by Japanese civilians after bailing out of the stricken plane. Two others, captured by the Japanese Kempei tai (secret police), failed to survive their first day of interrogation and captivity. One S/Sgt. Charles O. Baumgartner, of Sebring, Oh., the lower ball turret gunner, was imprisoned in Hiroshima.

Of the second Liberator, the *Lonesome Lady*, only one member of the nine-man crew was killed in the crash, apparently having been unable to bail out.

The survivors became prisoners of the Japanese, and seven of those eight were taken to Hiroshima for imprisonment and interrogation. One of the eight was captured and imprisoned elsewhere and thus survived the war as a POW. Another was transferred from Hiroshima to Tokyo for further interrogation and also survived as a POW.

The six remaining in Hiroshima were: 2nd/Lt. Durden Looper of Pine Bluff, Ark., the co-pilot; 2nd/Lt. James M. Ryan of Binghamton. N.Y., the bombardier; Sgt. Hugh H. Atkinson of Seattle, Wash., the radioman-gunner; Cpl. John A. Long, Jr., of New Castle, Pa., the nose gunner; S/Sgt. Ralph J. Neal of Corbin, Ky., the lower ball turret gunner.

Thus, nine American airmen were held in Hiroshima, where they suffered brutal interrogation by the Japanese who were determined to obtain details from them of the then expected U.S. invasion of the Japanese home islands. They remained there when the Enola Gay dropped the atomic bomb on the morning of August 6, 1945.

Six of the American POWs were either killed by the bomb

or angry Japanese on August 6, one survived until two days later, and two, who had tried to escape the intense heat by jumping into a cesspool, died of radiation illness on August 19, 1945.

The placement of a memorial tablet at the National Prisoner of War Museum August 5, 1989, at the Andersonville National Historic Site culminates several years of research by Michael Blair, a journalist from upstate New York, into the fate of the Americans killed at Hiroshima. He has served as chairman of the Hiroshima POW Memorial project.

Those assisting in the project included: [these names are mostly of those holding governmental positions; Gen. Colin Powell and Sen. Sam Nunn were included].

The memorial tablet was financed by a benefactor, who chose to remain anonymous.

# REFERENCES

Bernstein, Barton J. 1976. *The Atomic Bomb*. Boston: Little Brown.

Craig, William. 1967. *The Fall of Japan*. The Dial Press, (Penguin Books, 1979).

Craven, W. F. and J. F. Cate. 1948. *The Army Air Forces In World War II*. Vol. 5.

DeWalt, Gary. 1978. Genbaku Shi [Killed By The Atomic Bomb]. A documentary film. Santa Fe, NM: Public Media Arts.

Fujinaka, Teruko. 1997. *The Fallen B-24* (Translated by Akio Hoshino Lal). Privately reproduced.

Goodwin, Michael J. 1995. *Shobun, A Forgotten War Crime in the Pacific*. Mechanicsburg, PA: Stackpole Books.

Hanley, Fiske II. 1997. *Accused American War Criminal*. Austin, TX: Eakin Press.

Kaga, Otohiko (Translated by Ian Hideo Levy). 1982. *Riding the East Wind*. Tokyo: Kodansha International.

Kurzman, Dan. 1986. *Day Of The Bomb*. New York: McGraw-Hill.

Lehrer, Jim. 2000. *The Special Prisoner*. New York: Random House.

Martin, Malachi. 1988. *The Jesuits*. NY: Simon & Schuster.

Martindale, Robert M. 1988. *The 13th Mission*. Austin: Eakin Press.

Reynolds, C. G. 1968. *The Fast Carriers*. NY: McGraw-Hill.

Rogers, David. H. (Editor). 1996. *494th Bombardment Group (H) History WW II*. Copied for private distribution.

Ross, Walter R. 1995. *Courage beyond the Blindfold*. (Subtitled *The Last POWs of WW II*). Collierville, TN: Global Press.

Thomas, Gordon and M. M. Witts. 1977. *Enola Gay*. NY: Stein and Day.

Weintraub, Stanley. 1991. *Long Day's Journey Into War*. NY: Truman Talley Books-Dutton.